"You're Not in Kansas Anymore- The Life and Times of a Soldier in Japan: John Anderson Carriker, Jr.

S. David Carriker, D.Min. (1951-   )

ISBN: 0-936013-70-2

© 2014 by S. David Carriker. All rights reserved.

Heritage Publishing Company
7923 Waxhaw Hwy
Waxhaw, NC 28173
Web: www.HeritagePC.net
Mail: Heritage@carolina.rr.com

About the Author...

The Reverend S. David Carriker, D. Min., is a member of Charlotte Presbytery in the State of North Carolina. He Carriker earned a BA in Earth Science and Geography from the University of North Carolina at Charlotte [1975] and a Master of Divinity from Columbia Theological Seminary [1978]. He was then ordained in Fayetteville Presbytery in 1979 and later earned a Doctorate of Ministry from Columbia in 2002.

Dr. Carriker has served five churches in North Carolina and one in Virginia Beach, Virginia. He began writing in 1976 with **"The Carriker Family"** and has written numerous books on railroading and other historical subjects. He has also produced several videos, maps and charts on the railroading and church related subjects, past and present. He received a writer's award of 2003 from the North Carolina Presbyterian Historical Society for "Third Creek Presbyterian Church Cemetery: 1751-2000".

Dr. Carriker has four grown children, two grandchildren and a dog named Mickey! He enjoys railroad archeology, gardening, photography. His latest endeavors include a 'railroad garden' of 100+ year old artifacts, signs, unique items and signals.

RAILROAD Titles
Railroading in the Carolina Sandhills- Vol. 1-5
North Carolina Railroads
North Carolina Railroad Map
Electric Trolleys of North Carolina
Charlotte & Mecklenburg Co., NC Railroads & Depots
Salisbury, NC Railroading
Piedmont & Northern (Electric) Railway VIDEO
Aberdeen & Rockfish Railroad VIDEO
Laurinburg & Southern Railroad VIDEO
N&W Ry #1218: Through the Loops to Asheville VIDEO
Sandhills Shorties VIDEO
Railroading in Richmond County, NC
North Carolina Electric Railroads
The North Carolina Railroad in Charlotte, NC [NRHS]
4, 6 & 8 Cylinder Locomotives- Vol. 1

Mt. Mitchell Railroad: The Railroad in the Sky [pending]
Garysburg, NC Railroads [pending]
The North Carolina Railroad Compendium [pending]
Abraham Stevens and the First Railroad in NC [pending]
The Cash Story [SC] [pending]
The First 30 years of Railroading [1801-1831] [pending]
Early Railroads in the United States [pending]
Wilmington, Charlotte & Rutherford Railroad [pending]

OTHER Titles
The Geology of Richmond Co., NC [pending]
You're Not in Kansas Anymore: The Life and Times of
   A Soldier in Japan

FAMILY Titles
The Burnette & McLauchlin Family
The Carriker & Dorsey Family
The Ferguson & Henry Family
The Huffman & Mull Family
James Gay: A Man of Resolve
Ransom P. Cloud & The Carswells of Burke Co., NC
The Carriker Family
Jessie Kerr of Third Creek [pending]

CHURCH Titles
Third Creek Pres. Church Cemetery Photographs- CD
Population Figures of Rowan County, NC [1790-2000]
Third Creek Church Families, Vol. 1-6
18th Century Churches of Richmond Co., NC
Presbyterian Churches in Rowan Co., NC Records
Third Creek Pres. Church Cemetery Index: 1761-2000
250 Years of Spirituality at Third Creek Pres. Church
18th Century Churches in Rowan Co., NC
Third Creek Presbyterian Church Statistics
The NC Presbyterian Historical Society Program
Historic Third Creek [reprint]
Third Creek Histories: Vols. 1-4
Third Creek Families: Vol. 1-6
Mill Creek Church 1760-1880 [pending]
Third Creek Pres. Church Lists

Table of Contents

Introduction   Pages

Chapter 1:   John Anderson Carriker, Senior, [father]   2

Chapter 2:   Alma Elizabeth Dorsey, [mother]   7

Chapter 3:   Elizabeth Lois Carriker, [older sister]   13

Chapter 4:   Donald Malloy Carriker, [younger brother]   17

Chapter 5:   John Anderson Carriker, Junior   19

Chapter 6:   Military Service [1944-1946]   37

Chapter 7:   Merrell Berneice Mull, [wife]   205

Chapter 8:   John & Bernie after the War   211

Chapter 9:   A New Family   225

Chapter 10: Four Little Boys: sons John, III, David, Tim & Richard   233

Chapter 11: More Little Boys... and Girls!   251

       Grands: John, IV, David, Jr., Ashleigh, Jon, Bekah, Joseph,

          Jenny, Tim, Sarah

Chapter 12: And Great Grandchildren Too!   260

       Great Grands: Jack, Jonathan, Hannah, Anabel, Marcelo,

          Gabrielle

Chapter 13: One Plus One Equals Thirty-one   267

Appendix   273

Index   279

Introduction

This is a story in pictures. It contains more photographs than it does narrative, adding to the saying that 'a picture is worth a thousand words.' This story is about the life of John Anderson Carriker, Jr.

He was the son of a Presbyterian minister, who traveled all across the country proclaiming the love and grace of God. But before John Jr. was born, his father, John Sr., had a fascination of getting out and seeing the world. John Sr. had been raised [from 2-18] in Barium Springs orphanage, which gave him an eager desire to get out and see the country. After he graduated from the Barium Springs High School, he went to the nearby Davidson College and began to travel locally with friends to the neighboring areas. Then John Sr. went off to Louisville Seminary in Kentucky.

While learning in seminary, his desire to see the country became an opportunity- he could travel anywhere to minister to the people. John Sr. traveled to the people of Saskatchewan[1], Alberta[2] and British Columbia[3]. In the summer of 1918 he spent three months in preparation for war, headed to Europe for World War I, although, he never left this country.

He began ordained ministry by serving churches in Missouri[4], California[5] and Kentucky[6], prior to the birth of John, Jr. He and the family also made trips to visit family and friends in Montana, Minnesota and Ohio. By the time he arrived in Kansas[7], John, Sr. was now married and the little orphan boy and his new wife, Betsy, had their first two children: Betty and John, named after Betsy and Rev. John.

John Anderson Carriker, Junior was born in Kansas on August 12, 1925. He lived in West Virginia[8], Ohio[9] and Texas[10]. He then spent two years in the United States Army, mostly in Japan. His daily diary recounts his tales of living so far from home and is contained in this work. The diary has given me a new approach to my father and the life he experienced in the freshly destroyed country of Japan. He went overseas with the 369th Field Artillery Battery, an 155mm artillery regiment of the 98th Division. As the artillery was no longer needed, the military machinery was sent home, the 98th disbanded and a new priority was established:

---

[1] The Chapin family and the area of Neudorf, Saskatchewan, Canada
[2] Hunterville Presbyterian Church, Hunterville, Alberta, Canada
[3] Knox Presbyterian Church, Terrace, British Columbia, Canada
[4] First Presbyterian Church, Hopkins, Missouri
[5] First Presbyterian Church, Redding, California
[6] Elizaville Presbyterian Church, Elizaville, Kentucky
[7] First Presbyterian Church, Clifton, Kansas
[8] Weirton Presbyterian Church, Weirton, West Virginia
[9] Forest Lawn Presbyterian Church, Marion, Ohio
[10] Eldorado Presbyterian Church, Eldorado, Texas

rebuilding a broken country and people began. Dad was to spend much time in service to the Red Cross while he was there.

After the war, his parents had moved back to The Old North State [North Carolina!]. This was the area where the ancestry of both sides of the family came from. Rev. John had taken a two church field in Indian Trail[11] and Wesley Chapel[12] in Union County, NC for two years. Then he became an evangelist/church planter as an associate minister in Charlotte, NC[13]. He helped to establish two churches, one on the west side, near the airport[14] and one on the eastern outskirts of town[15]. The latter one became the church where he pastured until retirement.[16]

John Jr. began courting in the big city of Charlotte and there he soon found the love of his life, a young girl named Bernie. She, too, had been raised in a children's home, the Methodist Children's Home in Winston-Salem. And so his father and his new wife had orphanage and Children's Home background to bring to the new relationship. John and Bernie were married September 4, 1948 at the York County, SC courthouse and then came the family.

John Anderson Carriker, Jr. has now lived in Charlotte for 66 years. The new couple started out in an apartment on Morris Field Road in 1948, then built a house on 2800 Shenandoah Avenue in 1951, then built a house at 3300 Winterfield Place in 1964 and then built a house on 207 Kimrod Lane in 1972, where he lives today.

Here is his life in pictures. I hope you enjoy it. It is the story of our life too.

---S. David Carriker

---

[11] Indian Trail Presbyterian Church, Indian Trail, NC
[12] Siler Presbyterian Church, Wesley Chapel, NC
[13] Caldwell Memorial Presbyterian Church, Charlotte, NC
[14] Morris Field Presbyterian Chapel, Charlotte, NC
[15] East Side Presbyterian Chapel, Charlotte, NC
[16] Eastminster Presbyterian Church, Charlotte, NC

i

You're Not in Kansas Anymore

The Life and Times of a Soldier in Japan:
John Anderson Carriker, Jr.

By S. David Carriker
Waxhaw, North Carolina
2014

Chapter 1: John Anderson Carriker, Senior

The Reverend John A. Carriker, Sr., May 1976 at his home in Charlotte, NC.

John Anderson Carriker, Sr. [Nov. 3, 1892-Apr. 3, 1977] was the son of Alpha Lafayette Carriker [1867-Aug. 1894, above right] and Vernina Lenora Blackwelder [May 10, 1873-Oct. 1894]. They are buried to the right of the obelisk in unmarked graves at the cemetery of Rocky Ridge Methodist Church. There are no known photographs of Nina. John's grandfather, Adam Timothy Carriker, Jr. [1826-1882, no photo], is buried with them. John's Blackwelder grandparents are below: Columbus [Mar. 3, 1844-Jan. 3, 1918] and Esther Hartsell Blackwelder [Feb. 1, 1838-Feb. 2, 1924]. He is wearing a Southern Cross of Honor for his service in the Civil War. While John's parents died when he was two, he knew the Blackwelder grandparents and his Carriker grandmother! However, they all died before John, Jr. was born in 1925.

His grandmother, Jane Marie Owen Carriker [Dec. 14, 1841-Feb. 8, 1917] is pictured [above, left] and is buried at Rocky River Presbyterian Church. On the right is the home of Rev. John's parents when they died. John was born here and visited many times later in life. I saw it just before it was torn down in 1976. It stood at the lower inside corner of Zion Church Road and Mary Circle [above the current brick house]. Below are photos of John Sr. at age 4 and age 9 at Barium Springs Orphanage [Presbyterian] in Barium Springs, NC. His parents died when he was 2 and the aunts placed the John and his older sister, Sue, and younger brother, Alpha, Jr. in the nearest orphanage, Barium Springs, a new Presbyterian Orphanage. This is how the Carrikers moved from the Methodist and Lutheran Churches to the Presbyterian Church. He was there from 1896-1910 and went through 12 grades there. After graduation he went on to Davidson College for four years [1911-1915].

At Davidson College [1911-1915] he graduated with an A.B. degree and continued his studies at Louisville Theological Seminary where he received a B.D. The above photos were taken while he was a student at Davidson and the two below were taken while he was at the two schools [Davidson- 1912 and Louisville- 1918].

John Anderson Carriker, Sr. Timeline

Born: Nov. 3, 1892, nr. Concord, NC [nr. Harrisburg, NC]
father: Alpha Lafayette Carriker, Sr.; [died 1894]
mother: Vernina Lenora Blackwelder [died 1894]
wife: Alma Elizabeth Dorsey, Elizaville, KY, Feb. 14, 1922
chn: 1) Betty Lois Carriker (Mrs. Edmund B. Clark) 1923 [KS]
chn: 2) John Anderson Carriker, Jr. 1925 [KS]
chn: 3) Donald Malloy Carriker 1931 [OH]

Education:
- Barium Springs Orphanage [PCUS] {16 yrs.} 1895-1911 [attended Troutman PC]
- Davidson College [PCUS] {4 yrs.} 1911-1915, AB [attended Davidson College Chapel]
- Louisville Pres. Theo. Seminary [PCUS & UPC-USA] {3 yrs.} 1915-1918, BD [attended Seminary Chapel]

Ministry:
- visited Chapin family — 1916 — 1st sum.: visited friends: Neudorf, SK, CAN
- Presbyterian Church of Canada [PCC] — sum. pastor — 1917 — 2nd sum.: Hunterville PC, Hunterville, AB, CAN
- Presbyterian Church of Canada [PCC] — sum. pastor — 1918 — 3rd sum.: Knox PC, Terrace, BC, CAN

{Military:} US Army — sum-11/11/1918 [war ended]

Licensed: in Concord Presbytery [PCUS] — Nov. 15-30, 1918
Ordained: in St. Joseph Presbytery [UPC-USA] — July 1919 — Dism'd: 1919 to UPCUSA
installed 1919

Role	Location	Dates	Church	Notes
Pastor:	Hopkins, MO	1919-1920	First PC	
Pastor:	Redding, CA	1920-1921	First PC	Dism'd: 1921 to PCUS
Pastor:	Elizaville, KY	1921-1923	Elizaville PC	Dism'd: 1923 to UPCUSA
Pastor:	Clifton, KS	1923-1925	First PC	
Pastor:	Weirton, WV	1925-1927	Weirton PC and Weirton/Cove UPC merger	
Pastor:	Marion, OH	1927-1944	Forest Lawn PC	Dism'd: 1944 to PCUS
Pastor:	Eldorado, TX	1944-1946	Eldorado PC	
Pastor:	Union Co., NC	1946-1947	Siler PC & Indian Trail PC	
Assoc.:	Charlotte, NC	1947-1948	Caldwell Memorial PC [Morris Field Chapel]	
Planter:	Charlotte, NC	1947-1949	Caldwell Memorial PC [East Side Chapel]	
Planter:	Charlotte, NC	1949-1952	Caldwell Memorial PC [Eastminster Chapel]	
Pastor:	Charlotte, NC	1952-1961	Eastminster PC	
Supply:	[various]	May 30, 1961	[EPC merged with Commonwealth PC 5/3/1969]	
Landlord:	Montreat, NC	1961-1972	Mecklenburg Presbytery [excluding summers]	
Preach:	[various]	1972-1977	Mecklenburg House, (Texas Road Extension)	
			Mecklenburg Presbytery	

Rec'd: 1920 to Pres'y of Sacramento-San Fransisco
Transf.: 1921 in Ebenezer Pres'y
Rec'd: 1923 in Pres'y of Topeka-Wichita [UPC-USA]
Transf.: 1925 to Pres'y of Wheeling-Chippewa
Transf.: 1927 to Pres'y of Marion-Portsmouth
Rec'd: 1944 in Brown Pres'y [PCUS]
Transf.: 1946 Mecklenburg Pres'y
{Morris Field Chapel org. 5/1948}
{begun 1941; * (note below)}
{chapel moved to Chipley Ave. by truck}
{Org. 5/18/1952; Install 8/3/1952}

Honorably Retired

Died: April 3, 1977 in Charlotte, NC

: {in a tent-9/7/41; in two homes 10/41; frame building 1/42} {preached 60 yrs., supplied & preached: 58 yrs., pastored 42 yrs., 14 churches}
{ordained 58 years}

sources: Ministerial Directorcy of the PCUS, 1951, 1967, 1983; General Assembly Minutes and personal photos and notes of JAC, Sr.

Chapter 2: Alma Elizabeth Dorsey

Alma Elizabeth [Betsy] Dorsey Carriker

Sally Jane Howe [1785-1857] & John David Howe [1777-1853]
double- 1st cousins: [fathers David & John were brothers];
[mothers Sarah & Jane Dunlap were sisters]

The oldest photograph in existence within the family is this copy of the original portrait of Sally & John Howe. They died 1853-1857, so the photograph had to be taken prior to that. John David Howe was born March 30, 1777 in the old Waxhaw area in Lancaster Co., SC and died May 2, 1853 in Elizaville, KY. He was the son of John Howe and Jane Dunlap. Sally Jane Howe was born May 4, 1785 in the old Waxhaw area also, to David Howe and Sarah Dunlap. David and John Howe were brothers. Jane and Sarah Dunlap were sisters. John David Howe and Sarah Jane Howe Howe were therefore double-first cousins! Together, they had only two sets of grandparents.

Another set of ancestors on Betsy's side was the McIntyres, photographed about the same time as the Howes, in the early 1850's. There must have been a traveling photographer who went through Elizaville in the early 1850's. Both Duskin and Elisabeth were born around Washington, DC.

The third generation of Howes and McIntyres to be in Elizaville, KY was David Washington Howe and Margaret McIntyre. David Howe [June 12, 1812-Nov. 14, 1898] is the son of David & Sarah Howe. Margaret McIntyre [April 3, 1824-March 3, 1891] is the daughter of Duskin McIntyre and Elisabeth Darnell. They were both born Elizaville, KY and died there as well, before my grandmother was born in 1899.

Sarah Elizabeth Howe [left] was the daughter of David Washington Howe and Margaret McIntyre Howe. She was born June 2, 1866 and died September 16, 1944, both in Elizaville, KY. She married Samuel William Dorsey and is the mother of Alma Elizabeth Dorsey, who married John Anderson Carriker, Sr. She has her mother's distinct eyes. She died 7 years prior to my birth, but I did meet her husband, Samuel, who was my great grandfather.

Frances Sarah Strode was born June 30, 1839 and died June 5, 1908. She lived her entire life in Elizaville, KY and is buried there.

William Ingram Dorsey was born in 1833 and died December 25, 1913. He lived his entire life in Elizaville, KY and is buried there.

Their son was Samuel William Dorsey who was born May 30, 1862 and died January 13, 1953 in Elizaville, KY. He held me as a toddler in 1952. Both Samuel and Sarah are buried in the Elizaville Cemetery, near the old home place where they lived for so long. They are the grandparents of John Anderson Carriker, Junior.

Alma Elizabeth Dorsey is 16 in this photo of about 1915. She was the daughter of Samuel and Sarah Dorsey.

Seen in this photo from March 1926, soon after the Carrikers arrived in Clifton, KS is a young Betsy Carriker, age 26.

Rev. John Carriker is 34 in this photo from March, 1926.

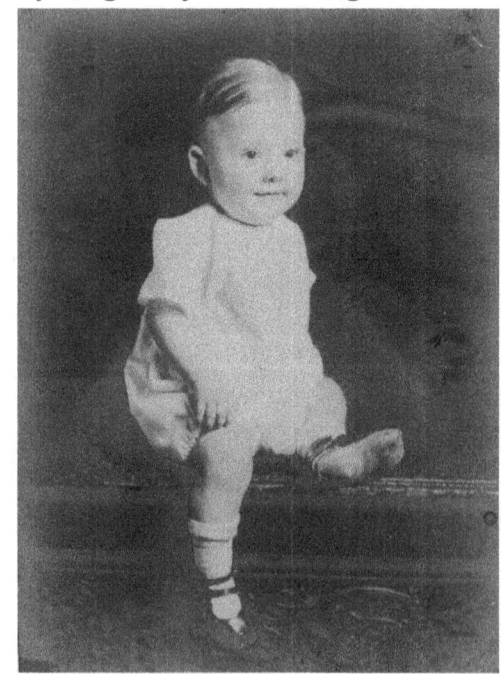

Little Jack Carriker [John, Jr.] is just seven months old in March 1926.

Chapter 3:   Elizabeth Lois Carriker

Elizabeth Lois Carriker was born November 27, 1923 in Clifton, Kansas to John and Betsy Carriker, Sr. She is the older sister of John Carriker, Jr. and his younger brother, Donald Malloy Carriker. Her mother was called 'Betsy' and she was called 'Betty,' both of which are nicknames for Elizabeth.

Betsy was named by her mother, Sallie, in memory of her grandmother, Elizabeth Darnell. She had died when Sallie was 14 [1880] and Sallie remembered her grandmother in 1899 when Betsy was born and named her daughter after her grandmother.

Betsy passed the name on to Betty in 1923 and Betty passed the name to her daughter in 1950, Laura Elizabeth Clark.

In 1924, the Carrikers were on their way up north in Minnesota to go camping with friends. They stopped along the way to take this photo of Betty, sitting on the back of the folded roof top. Betsy can barely be seen holding her from behind while she hides in the back seat!

Betty is carrying her baby-doll, while she and Jack make their way up the back steps of their home in Clifton, Kansas prior to moving to Weirton, West Virginia.

A young Betty Carriker in Marion, OH with her brother John Carriker, Jr.

Betty Carriker Clark and Bernie Mull Carriker in the mid 1950's in Charlotte, NC

Betty Carriker Clark from a series of family photos taken about 1956 at her parents' home in Monroe Road in Charlotte, NC. The home was the manse of the Eastminster Presbyterian Church, located two blocks around the corner. It was the home of many fond memories for the family.

Carol Ann Clark [above- b. 10/5/1946] was the first child of Betty Carriker & Edmund Burke Clark, Jr. and Laura Elizabeth Clark [right- b. 2/4/1950] was the second child.

Chapter 4: Donald Malloy Carriker

A young Don Carriker, with his parents, Betsy and John Carriker in Marion, OH. Don was born December 29, 1931, about six years after John Jr., in Marion, OH.

Don Carriker in the mid 1950's is looking real sharp! By this point he is living in Charlotte, but in school at UNC in Chapel Hill, where he will meet Lolly Barefoot.

Don was named after Mr. Donald Malloy, a man who took a personal interest in Rev. John Carriker while he was in school. Three generations of Carrikers are here: Rev. John Sr., his sons: John Jr., and Don, and one grandson, David. The photo was taken on the front porch of the manse on Monroe Road in Charlotte, NC while Rev. Carriker was the pastor at Eastminster Presbyterian Church.

Kimberley Diane Carriker [center, b. 5/8/1961] was the first child of Don and Loretta [Lolly] Jean Barefoot Carriker. Michael Anderson and Jeffrey Stewart Carriker were twins borns May 12, 1964.

Chapter 5: John Anderson Carriker, Junior

John Jr. and "Lucky" headed down the Grand Canyon trail- 2005

John Jr. was born [August 12, 1925] while his father served the Clifton Presbyterian Church in Clifton, Kansas.

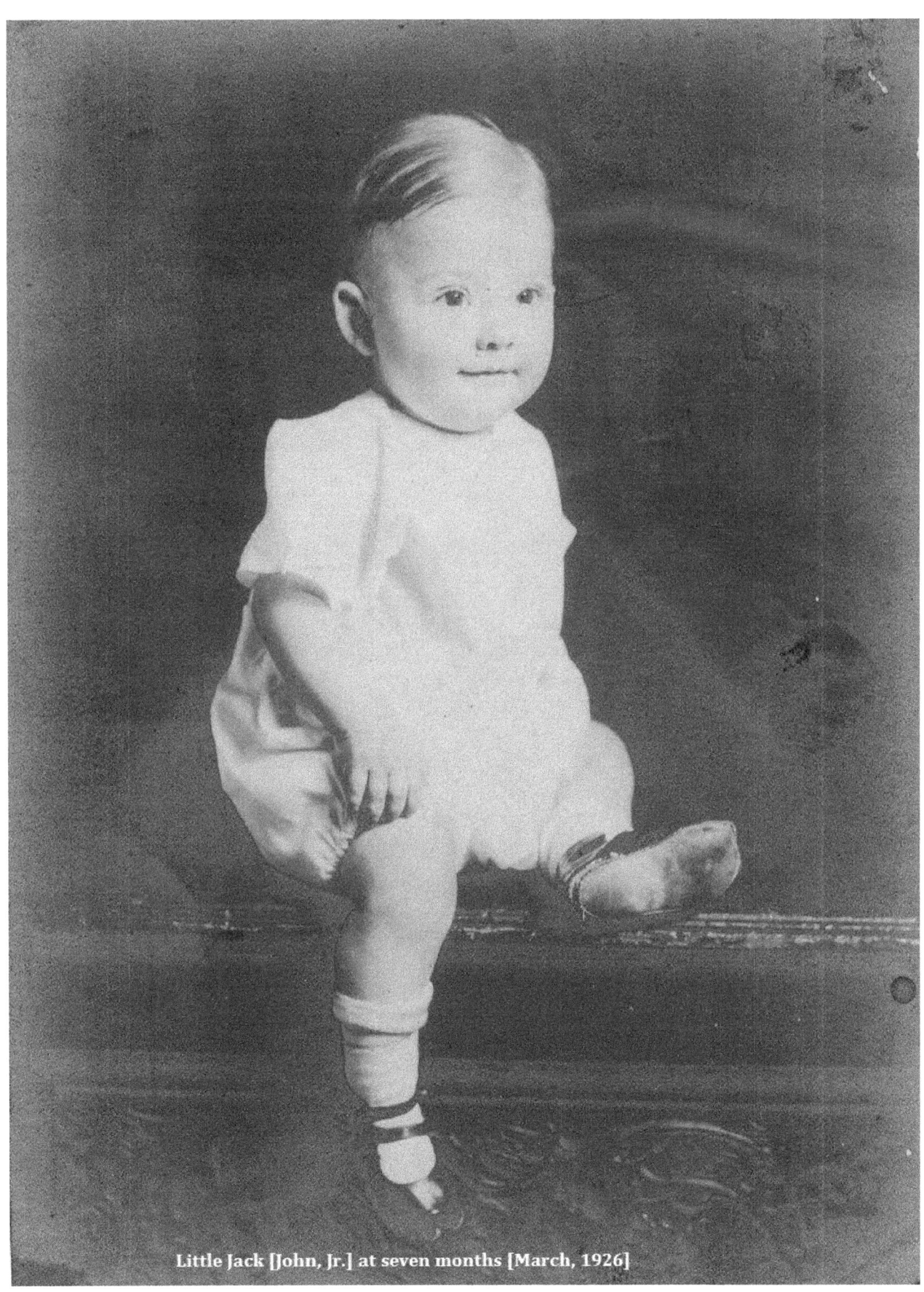
Little Jack [John, Jr.] at seven months [March, 1926]

The Carrikers had just moved to Weirton, WV when this photo was taken.

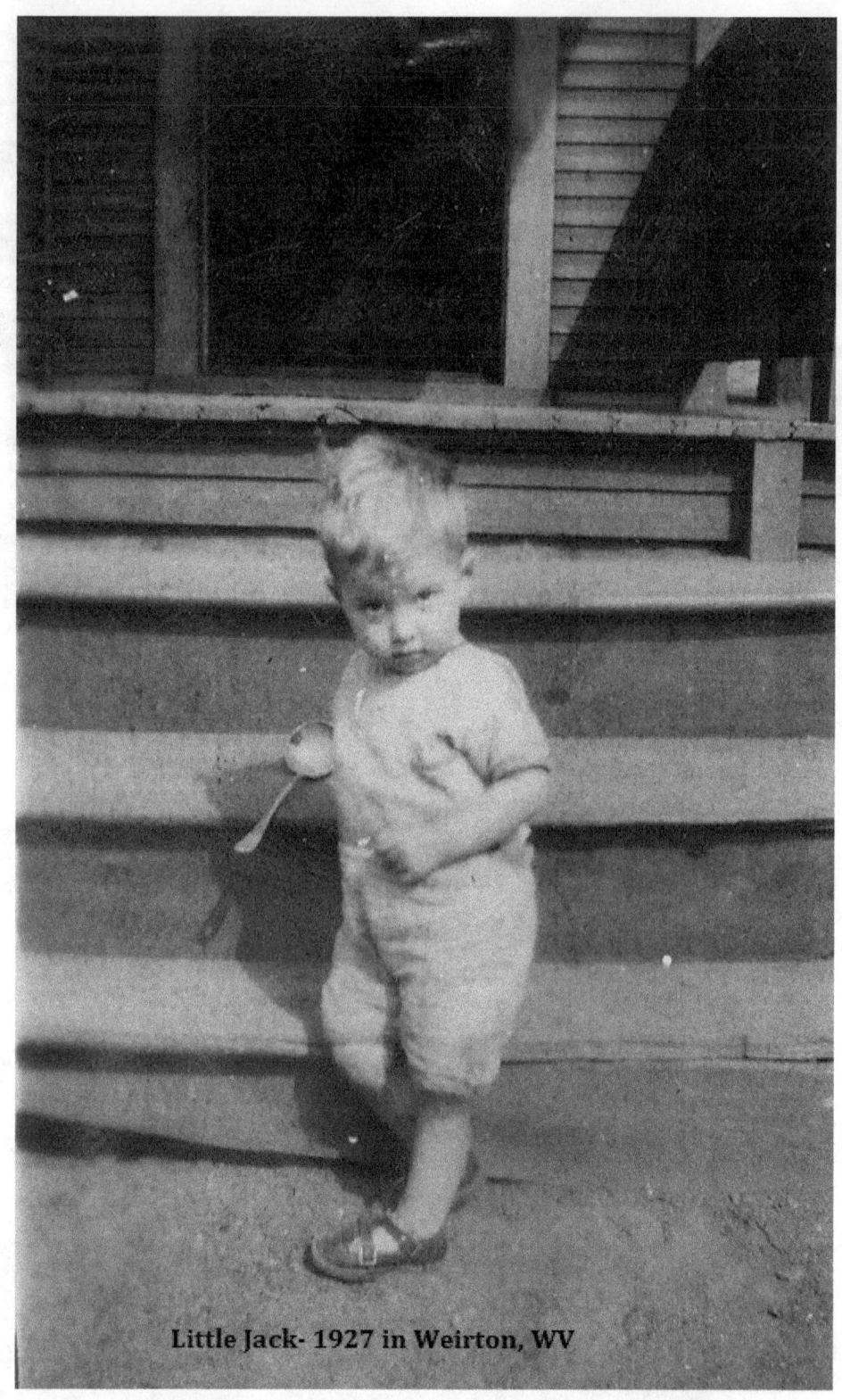
Little Jack- 1927 in Weirton, WV

Mischievous was always a Carriker look,
even when we are innocent and someone else was guilty.

A boy and a spoon to play with... what could possibly go wrong!?

3 year old Jack in Marion, OH

Jack is in stockings riding a tricycle.

1929- Forest Lawn Presbyterian Church, Marion, OH

The Carrikers moved to Marion, Ohio in 1927
and lived there for seventeen years.

119 Johnson St., Marion, Ohio

This was the Carriker home in Marion, Ohio during a winter snowstorm.

Jack and Betty playing on 119 Johnson St. in Marion.

Marion, Ohio was a railroad town!

The Railroads of Marion, Ohio

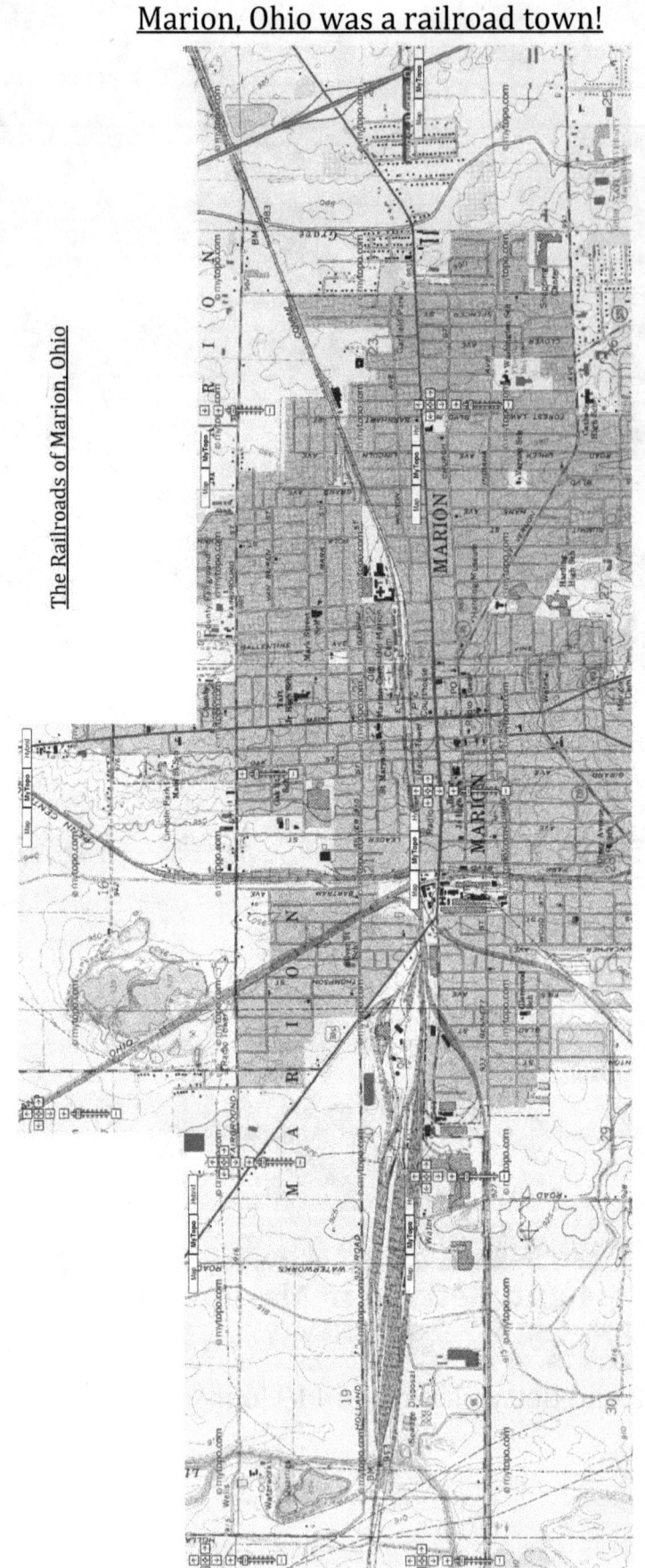

Four railroads, a train yard, a roundhouse, a turntable and dozens of trains everyday. Marion is a railroad town.

This is a happy family.
Notice Betsy's gloved hand holding little Jack still!
They made regular visits to Elizaville, KY,
which was only a few hours from Marion, Ohio.

Jack Jr. [right] at his Kindergarten Graduation.

One popsicle; two kids!

Growing up in Marion, Ohio in 1935.

Together for a wonderful Elizaville Day
Celebrating the Golden Wedding Anniversary
Of Samuel William and Sally Howe Dorsey-
November 20, 1940!

John, Jr. at 16 [1941] in Marion, OH

The photos of a teenager.

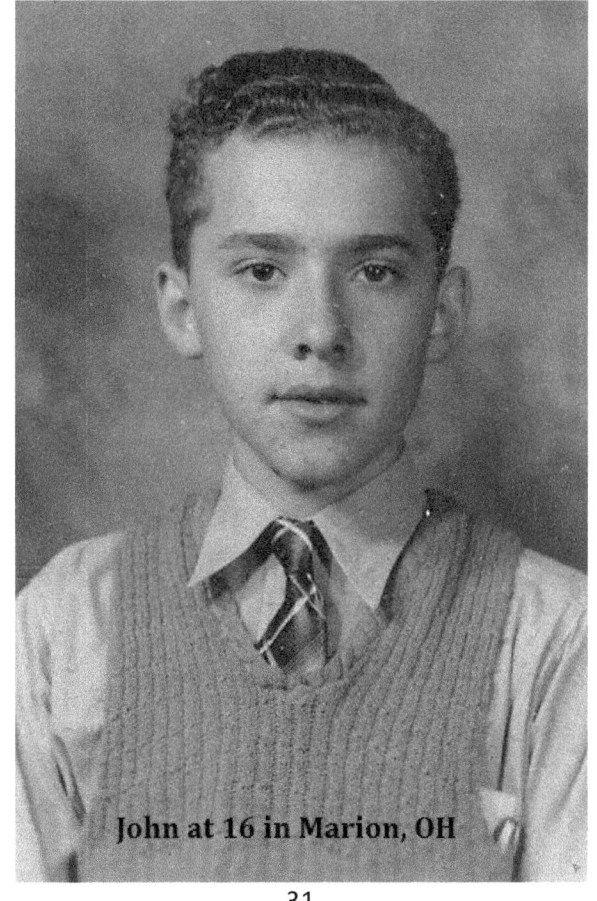
John at 16 in Marion, OH

Annie, Jack, Betsy, Estelle, Don, Dorothy Jane at Bat Cave in 1942

The Taylor's inherited the property at Bat Cave.
It was a fun place to visit and a good source for apples!

John at 17 in 1942

Getting ready to graduate
from High School
... and go to War!

The 15th of 17 years in Marion.
John Jr. [17], Betsy [42], Don [11], John Sr. [50], Betty [19]
representing 24 years of ministry!

1943 graduation photo, John in Marion, OH

1943 graduation at Johnson St. home in Marion, OH

After graduation, John worked for the Erie Railroad in Marion, Ohio as a Signal Maintainer's Assistant. He filled kerosene oil lamps on switch stand lamps and signals for 9 months in 1944.

1944- Don, Jack, Betsy & Rev. John, Sr. in Eldorado, TX

Missing Marion, OH but looking ahead to new ministry in Texas.

1945- First Presbyterian Church, Eldorado, TX

Chapter 6:   Military Service [1944-1946]

Introduction

John Carriker, Jr. grew up quickly. He had lived with his parents in the comfort of his family for all of his life. He graduated from Marion High School in May 1943 [17¾], worked for the Erie Railroad in Marion for nine months [April-December, 1943], move to Eldorado, Texas and enrolled in Texas Christian University [January, 1944] and joined the US Army December 26, 1944 [19¼]. Life also changed quickly as the world was at war and now he was of the age to be drafted. Japan was on the horizon and John would eventually head there for a life-changing story in his young life. One of the place he visited was Yokohama…

Pre-War Japan

An unknown "House #9" in Yokohama in 1900.

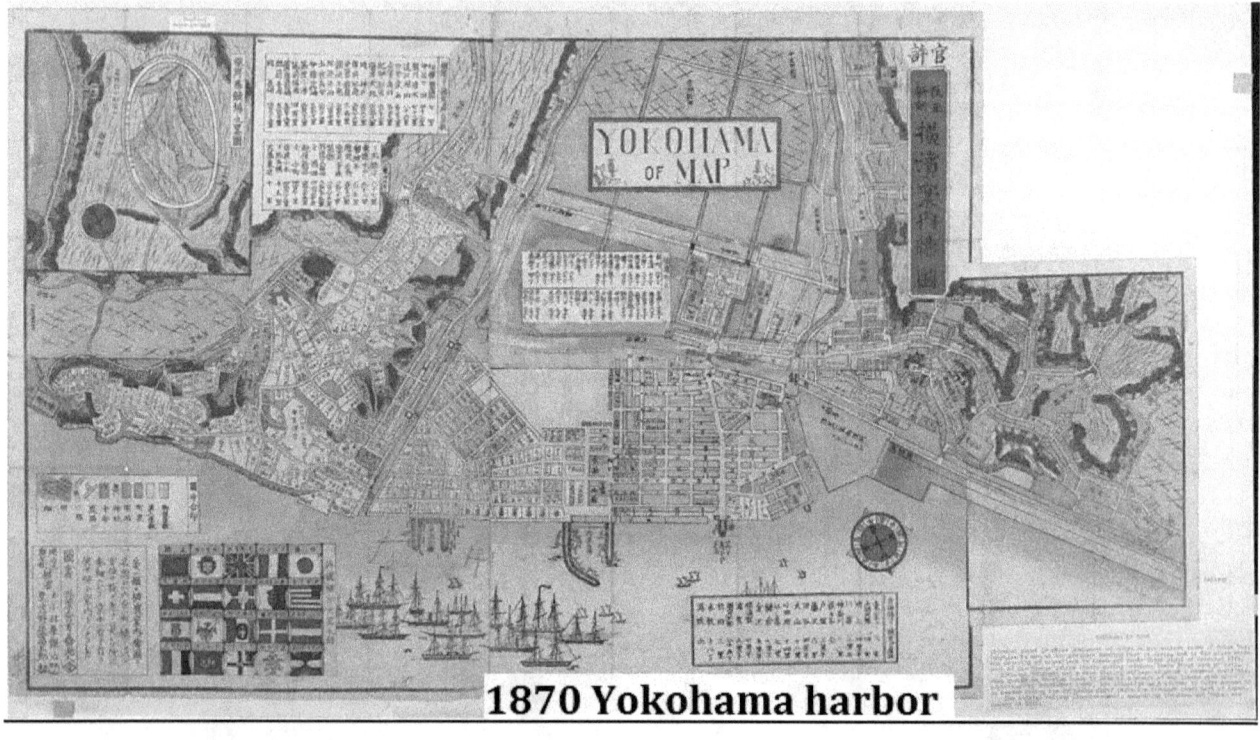

1866 Yokohama

1870 Yokohama harbor

1871 Yokohama steam

1871 Yokohama

1873- Kamakura Diabutsu

1880 Samurai family in Yokohama

[see description on next page]

1880 Samuri in Yokohama

1904 Yokohama big sisters and little brothers

1881-1900 Yokohama street scene

Postcard 1900 Daibutsu Temple in Nara- bt in 734 AD under Emporer Shomu

Postcard 1900 Daibutsu Buddha in Nara- bt in 734 AD

Postcard 1900 Daibutsu Lantern in Nara

1900 Daibutsu Temple in Nara- bt. in 734 AD under Emporer Shomu

1900 Daibutsu Temple in Nara

Postcard Hachiman Shrine at Kamakura

Postcard Maiko or dancing girls of Kyoto in Japanese Kimono

Postcard- Mandarin Orange trees are planted in terraces reaching from the foot tot he peak of a hill

Postcard- Mount Fuji- Fujiyama or Fuji-san is the highest mountain in Japan. The Japanese entertain a sort of devotion to her.

Fujiyama from Numagawa

1900 Nara Temple Bell and attendant

Temmoji Buddhist Temple in Osaka 1900

Temple entrance at Nara

1900 Temple in Nara

1900- Another Temple in Nara

1900 Temple in Nara

1900 Yokohama houses

1900 Yokohama men

1900 Yokohama snow

1900 Yokohama Sumo wrestlers

1900 Yokohama street

This is what awaited John Carriker: the American surrender of Manila in 1942 by General Jonathan Wainwright, IV to General Tomoyuki Yamashita on May 6, 1942. This was no longer a matter of the safety of the Philippines, or the people within the country. Now a three-star United States general was being held captive, along with a hundred thousand soldiers. So off to the war John went.

1942 Wainwright surrendering to Yamashita in Manila

The Diary of John Anderson Carriker, Jr.

Citations, Awards and Decorations

   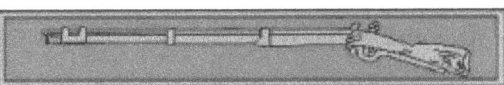

Sharpshooters Medal	Pacific Theatre Ribbon	American Theater Ribbon	Expert Infantryman Badge
4/15/1945	8/3/1945	8/3/1945	8/6/1945

   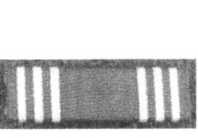

Drivers Medal	Japan Occupation Ribbon	Victory Medal	Good Conduct Ribbon
9/27/1945	9/27/1945	11/22/1946	11/22/1946

Ranks

7th Grade	6th Grade	5th Grade	
No Insignia	(chevron)	(chevron with T)	
Private	Private First Class	Technician Fifth Grade	
Pvt.	Pfc.	T/5.	
Private	Private 1st Class	Corporal, Tech 5	Discharged
12/26/1944	8/28/1945	12/10/1945	11/22/1946

My Life in the Service-   John Anderson Carriker, Jr.

Service Record	Dates
Sworn in at Fort Sam Houston, Texas	
Rank: **Private**	Dec. 26, 1944 – Jan. 6, 1945
At Camp Hood, Texas	Jan. 6, 1945 – Apr. 17, 1945
[home in Eldorado, Texas]	April 17, 1945 – May 5, 1945
At Fort Meade, Maryland	May 5, 1945 - June 26, 1945
At Fort Lawton, Washington	June 26, 1945 – July 2, 1945
On the S.S. Julian [Liberty troop ship]	July 2, 1945 – July 10, 1945
At 13th Rd. on Oahu, Hawaii	July 10, 1945 – July 13, 1945
At Waianae, Oahu, Hawaii [Amphibious training]	July 13, 1945 – July 16, 1945
At Helemano, Oahu, Hawaii [Weapons training]	July 16, 1945 – July 24, 1945
At Punaluu, Oahu, Hawaii [Jungle training]	July 24, 1945 – Aug. 21, 1945
At Fort Hose, Hawaii	Aug. 21, 1945 – Aug. 27, 1945
Promotion: **Private 1st Class**	Aug. 28, 1945 - Sept. 6, 1945
On S.S. Cape Johnson [Liberty troop ship]	Sept. 7, 1945 – Sept. 19, 1945
Saipan	Sept. 19, 1945 – Sept. 21, 1945
On S.S. Cape Johnson [Liberty troop ship]	Sept. 22, 1945 – Sept. 27, 1945
Landed at Wakayama Beach, Japan	Sept. 27, 1945
To Taisho airfield, Japan	Sept. 27, 1945 – Oct. 14, 1945
To Nara, Japan	Oct. 14, 1945 – Nov. 19, 1945
A few weeks [driving] Osaka, Koriyama,	Nov. 19, 1945 – Dec. 10, 1945
Tanbrach, Yogi, & Tsu	
Promotion: **Corporal Tech 5th Grade**	Dec. 10, 1945
Tsu, Matsusake, Suzuka, Toba, Nagoya, Ozakai	Dec. 26, 1945 – Feb. 10, 1946
Tokyo & Yokohama	Feb. 10, 1946 – [Sept. 13, 1946]
[On S.S. Norway Victory {Victory troop ship}]	[Sept. 13, 1946 – Sept. 26, 1946]
[Yokasura, Japan to Seattle, WA]	
[Seattle, WA to Washington, D.C. by train]	[Sept. 26, 1946 – Oct. 1, 1946]
[Washington, D.C. to Fort Bragg, NC by train]	[Oct. 1, 1946 – Oct. 2, 1946]
[at Fort Bragg, NC]	[Oct. 2, 1946 – Oct. 7, 1946]
[Fort Bragg, NC to Sanford, NC by taxi]	[October 7, 1946]
[Sanford, NC to Charlotte, NC, by bus, 10:30pm]	[October 7, 1946]
[Charlotte, NC]	[Oct. 7, 1946-Nov. 22, 1946]
[Charlotte, NC- discharged]	[November 22, 1946]

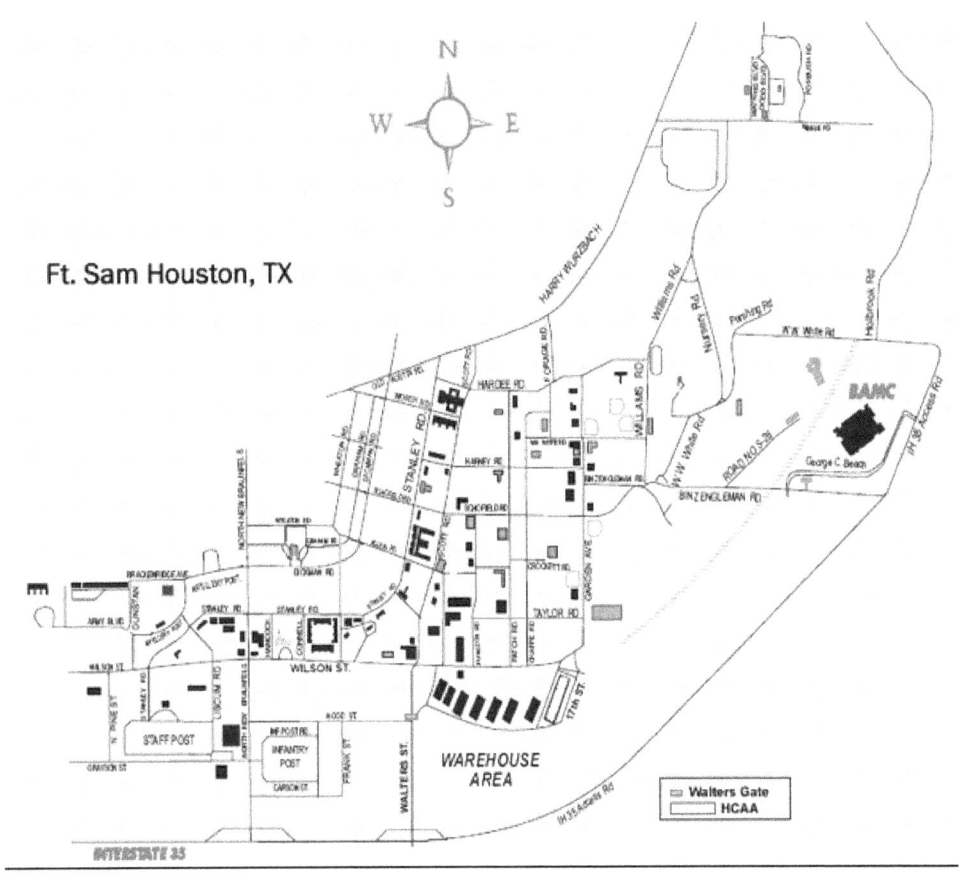

Ft. Sam Houston, TX

1944-12 Gamma, Jack & Don Carriker in Eldorado, TX

My Buddies	Hometown
Clarence Engel	Amboy, MN
Leo C. Devine	RFD #3 Howell, MI
Gene Carriker	Caney, KS
Philip Jenkins	San Antonio, TX
Leonard Hohenberger	San Antonio, TX
James Butler	Dallas, TX
Howard Crainley	Timpson, TX
Bob Christensen	Chicago, IL
Clements Chnooski	Chicago, IL
John Harrington	Kansas City, MO
Howard Carman, USN	Kinlon, PA
Stewart Hamilton	Marion, OH
John Patterson	Marion, OH
Bill O'Neil	Marion, OH
Sgt. Lattimore	Camp Hood, TX
Bud Hare	Virginia
Donal Yegge	
Hosley Walters	
Bob Trehka	Minnesota

Officers I Knew

Capt. Seale Mathews	Co. B, 176th Btn, 96th Regt., Camp Hood, TX
Lt. Louis Wooten	Co. B., 175th Btn, 96th Regt., Camp Hood, TX [Rock Hill, SC]
Maj. W. Zimmer	369th Field Artillery Btn., APO 98, Columbus, OH
Capt. Handell	Harrison Ave., Cincinnati, OH
Maj. Simon	Chicago, IL
Capt. Daly	
Lt. Orr	

Civilians I Met

Mary Gene [Candy] Handy	met her in Forth Worth at TCU; Grant Lindu & I double-dated
Dorothy Smith	[TCU] met at service club at Camp Hood
Mary Turner	Washington, DC: met Mary at Glen Echo Park
Gloria Baldison	Met Gloria at Earle Theatre in Washington, DC
Kataki	Nora, Japan
Katsu Ha	"
Tomi	"
Miss Ruth Meehon	Red Cross transportation officer, Washington, DC
Greta	Canteen girl
Virginia Slegle	Charlotte, NC
Mary Brochowler	NY
Sis Lucas	Boston, MA
Anita	Boston, MA
Pat Smith	Virginia
Miss Todd	Boston, MA

Dates to Remember

Nov. 9	Ruth Hay- birthday
Nov. 17	Mary Ann Sawyer- birthday
Nov. 3	Dad- birthday
Dec. 3	Mom- birthday
Nov. 27	Sis [Betty]- birthday
Dec. 29	Don- birthday

Camp Hood, Texas

1944-12 John Carriker Sr & Jr in Fort Hood, Texas

Places I Have Been

San Antonio, TX	The little river running through the downtown district
Fort Worth, TX	Ice skating at TCU
Old Mexico	The little town- the high and low prices
Detroit, MI	The river city- free street cars
Washington, DC	Smithsonian Museum, Monument, Glen Echo Park, Gloria, Mary
	The Presbyterian Church crowd
On a troop train	Baltimore to Seattle, Washington [bleak] to Montana [beautiful streams]
Washington	Mountains and lakes
Fort Lawton	Beautiful view
S.S. Julian	The blue Pacific
Honolulu, HI	high prices, Hula girls
Waikiki Beach	pineapple factory
Waianae Beach	natives in village
Pali Pass on Oahu	the beaches
Ft. Hall	Kajabea
Sheffield barracks	Hickman Field
Pearl Harbor	
Punaluu **USO**	cute girl there [mixture]
S.S. Cape Johnson	from Honolulu to Saipan to Wakayama, Japan
To Osaka to Nara to Tsu to Nagoya to Okazaki to Kyoto, Yokohama, Tokyo	
	Taisho Air Field [Osaka]- Kamakura, Enoshima

Examined at Dallas, TX
Was at San Antonio, TX, Austin, Ft. Worth to San Angelo and Camp Hood, TX
Train to Arkansas, Missouri, Illinois, Indiana, Ohio, Michigan, Pennsylvania, Delaware, Maryland, Washington, DC, Iowa, Minnesota, Wisconsin, North Dakota, South Dakota, Montana, Idaho, Washington State, Hawaii, Saipan and Tinian Islands. Then to the Japanese Islands, Wakayama, Osaka, Kobe, Kyoto, Taisho Air Field, Nara, Tsu, Toba, Matsusaka, Suzuki, Nagaya, Okasaki, Yokohama, Tokyo, Kamakura, Enoshima.

Texas Christian University, Ft. Worth, Texas

Camp Meade, Maryland

Letters Received

Don	Dec. 16, Jan. 10, Mar. 19
Ann	Dec. 23, Feb. 9
Uncle Cecil	Dec. 23, Mar. 10
Mrs. Dugan	Dec. 16
Aunt Mabel	Dec. 16
Aunt Annie	Dec. 16
Mary Ann S.	Dec. 23, Jan. 15, Jan. 27, Feb. 7, Feb. 10, Mar. 10, Mar. 19, Mar. 31, May 7, May 19
Ruth Hay	Dec. 23
Ruth Bull	Dec. 22, Dec. 23, Feb. 10, March 8
Aunt Sue	Dec. 22, Feb.15, April 7
Norma B.	Dec. 24
Red Cross	Jan. 6
R.I. Almer	Dec. 24
Mary Ann Turner	June 8
June	Jan. 13
Grant	Jan. 11, Jan. 21
Tinsy	Dec. 24, Feb. 17, Feb. 20, Mar. 21, Mar. 31, April 6, April 21, May 1
Gene Carriker	Jan. 15
Jean Houghton	Jan 5, April 11, May 10
Cowart	Jan. 21
Skippy	Mar. 21, Mar. 31, April 7
Mary Brochowler	Mar. 21, May 8

Mt. Fujiyama at end of war

Glen Echo Park Dance Floor

Glen Echo Park, Maryland

Diary Explanation
[bracketed items: notes]   boxed items are added important events
All media are in bold quotations [shows, movies, songs].

The Diary   [text]

> *[The Battle of the Bulge began just 10 days prior to John's enlistment.*
> *The Battle ended on the day of his enlistment]*

December 26, 1944   I left Eldorado, Texas the day after Christmas 1944 at 12 noon. The bus ride was rainy to San Antonio. *[age: 19⅓ years]*

December 27, 1944   I was sworn in at Fort Sam Houston, Texas.

[December 28, 1944-January 2, 1945   no dated entry]

January 3, 1945   I had two passes to go to San Antonio. After one week I went to Camp Hood, Texas and spent 16 weeks there taking all sorts of absentees, learning weapons on maneuvers. We lost five boys when bridge broke [over a flooded river; the bodies were found one mile down river]. Our camp had 65,000 men. I had 8 or 10 weekend passes, through to Eldorado, a couple at camp, the rest at TCU in Fort Worth with Grant Lindu.

[January 4, 1945- April 16, 1945   no dated entry]

> *[US Marines invaded Iwo Jima on 2/19. It was secure in 4 weeks.*
> *Major fire bombings in Japan:*
> *   Tokyo 3/9-10; Nagoya 3/11; Osaka 3/13; Kobe 3/16; Nagoya 3/19; Tokyo 4/7 & 4/15; Kawasaki 4/15; Yokohama 4/15.*
> *US Army invaded Okinawa on 4/1 in the last major amphibious assault.*
> *President Roosevelt died on April 12]*

April 17, 1945   I got my furlough from April 17th to May 9th and spent the time at home for 10 days in Eldorado, TX. I left on Wed. night from San Angelo [TX]. I had an awful time saying goodbye to Mom and Dad and Don. Never want to have to do that again. Stopped in Ft. Worth [TX] for about 6-8 hours at TCU. Got in Marion, OH Friday night about 6:00pm; went to Jim Houghton's house (wonderful time); went uptown with Jim to Club Co-Ed. Jane was beautiful. Kids all glad to see me. Left Sat. morning at 4:00am for Detroit, Michigan. Mrs. Crizie Grace and Norma (supremely beautiful) were with me. Saw sis & Ed till Tuesday.

[April 18, 1945-May 7, 1945   San no dated entry]

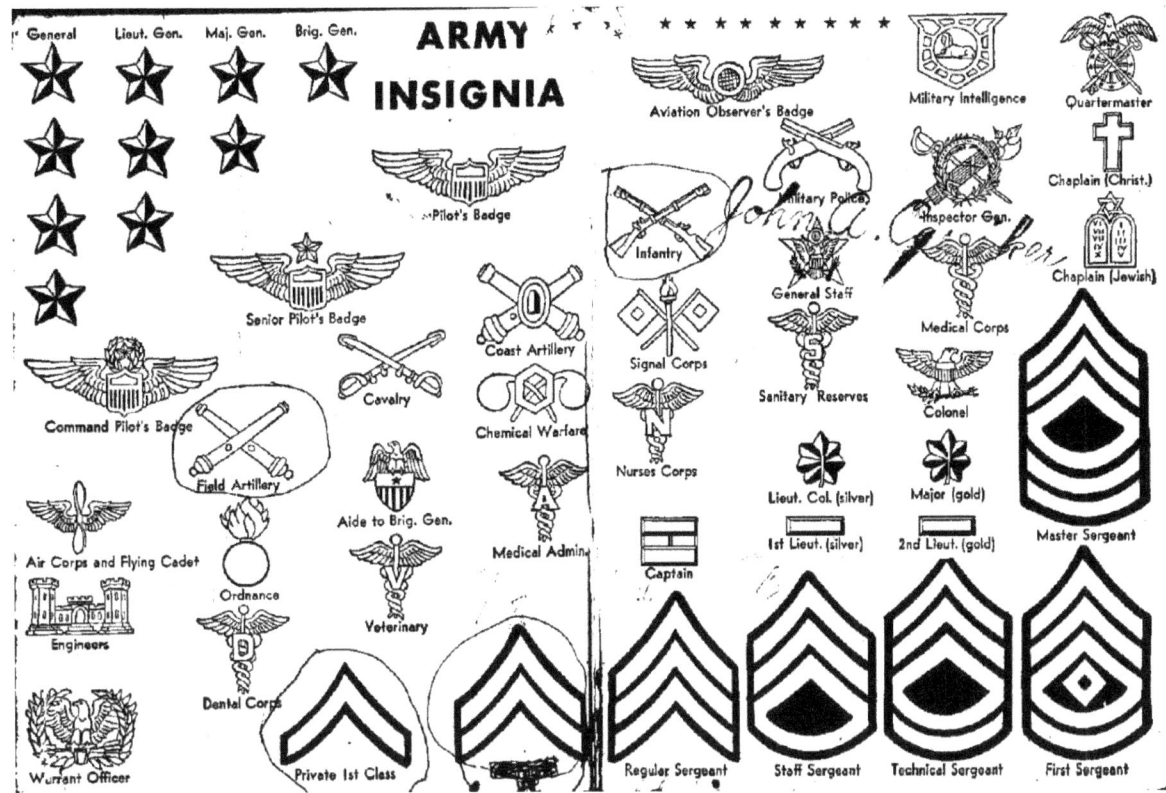

The Army Insignia page for easy recognition

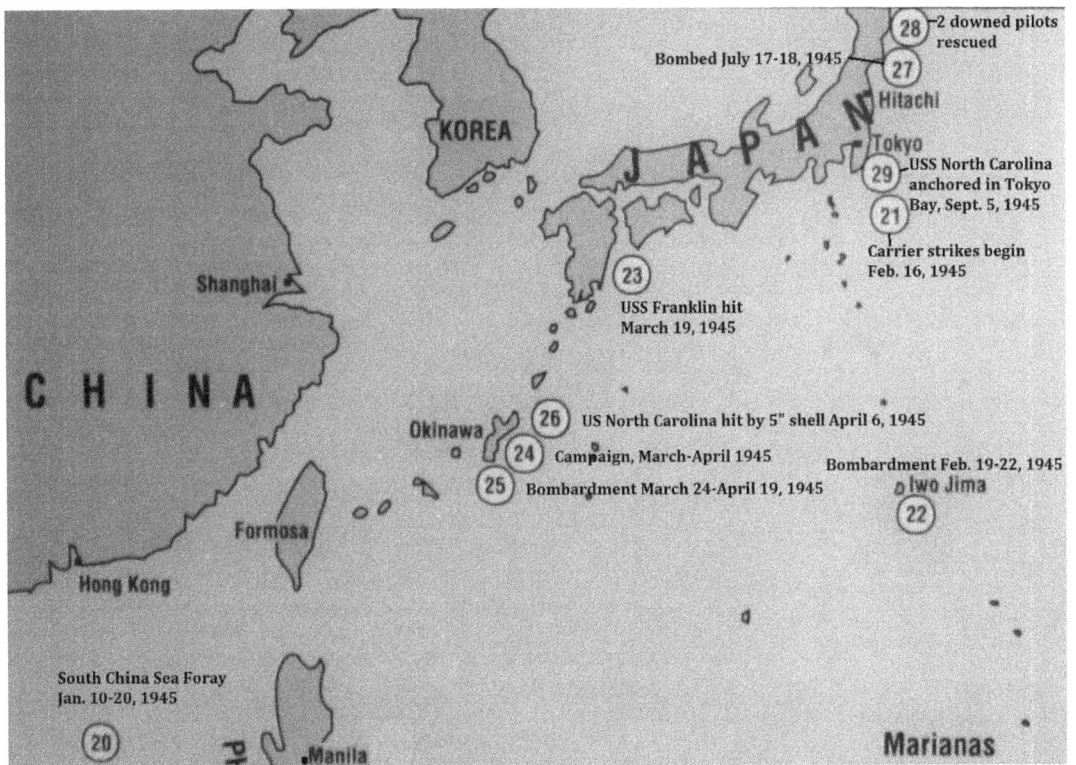

The Steps to Japan by the battleship USS North Carolina

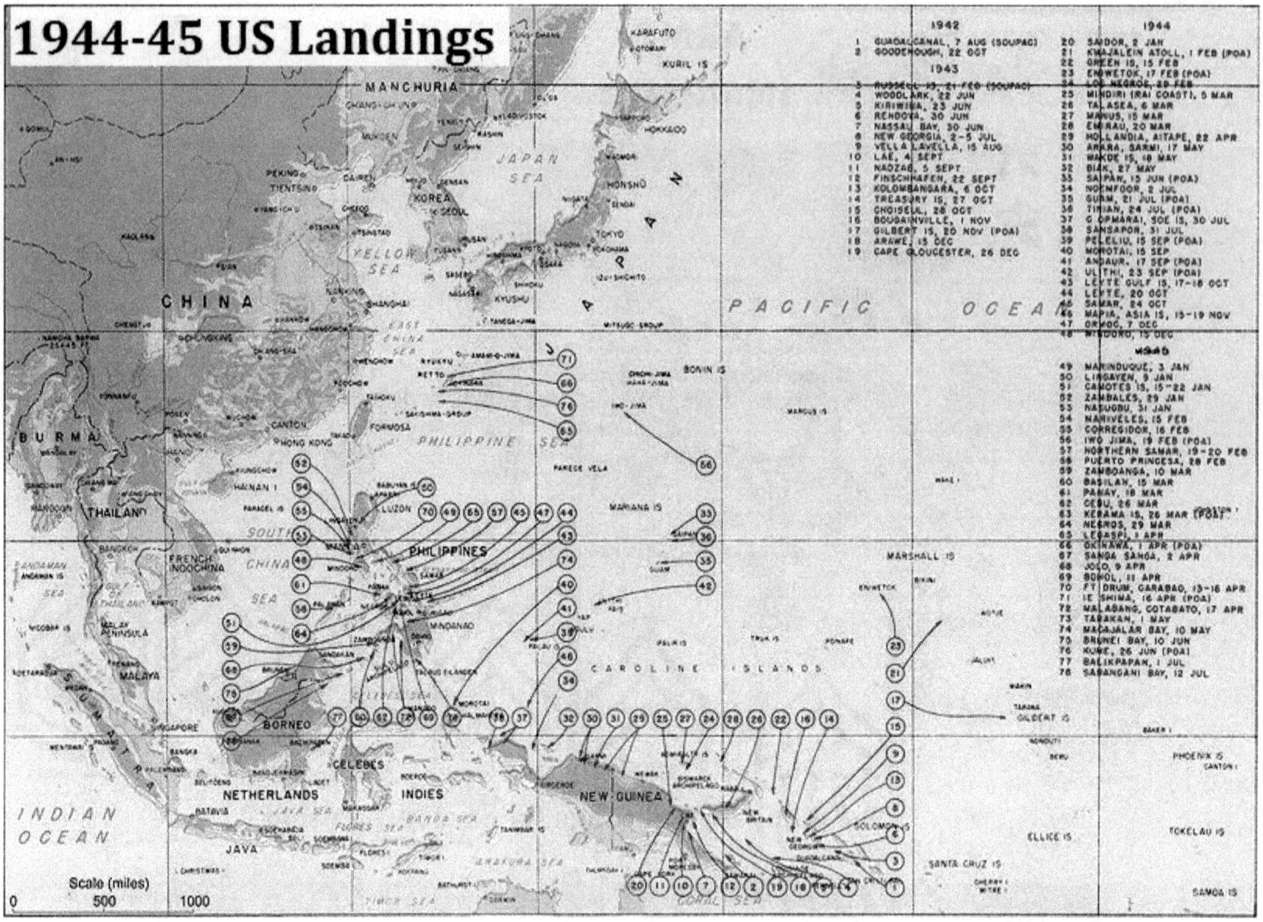

1944-45 US Landings

A 1945 B-29 used on a bombing run

Fort Lawton, Seattle, Washington

The restored S.S. John W. Brown liberty ship [similar to the S.S. Julian]
2,711 Liberty Ships [EC-2] were built and named for prominent Americans 1941-1944.
Two are restored as museums; 200 were lost to torpedoes, mines or kamikazis.

> *April 1945   Allied forces begin to take 2.4 million German & Italian prisoners.*
> *April 25, 1945 The last Germans were expelled by the Finnish Army from Finland.*
> *April 27, 1945 Italian dictator Benito Mussolini was captured by Italian partisans and executed the next day in Giulino*
> *April 29, 1945 SS General Karl Wolff surrendered at Caserta, Italy. Nearly 1,000,000 men in Italy and Austria surrendered to British Gen. Harold Alexander at 2pm.*
> *April 30, 1945 Adolf & Eva Hitler committed suicide in his Führerbunker at 3:30pm.*
> *May 1, 1945   Joseph Goebbels, the new chancellor of Germany for only 29 hours, committed suicide at 8:15pm.*
> *May 2, 1945   The Battle of Berlin ended.*
> *May 4, 1945   German forces in NW Germany, Denmark, the Netherlands & Bavaria surrender.*
> *May 6, 1945   Hermann Göring's surrender.*
> *May 7, 1945   President Dönitz ordered Gen. Jodl and Gen. Keitel to surrender all German armed forces unconditionally at 11:01pm.*
> *May 8, 1945   Victory in Europe*
> *May 8 – September 4, 1945   "German holdout" units cease fire on May 8, 9, 12, 13, 15, 16, 20 and September 4.*

May 8, 1945   at 5:30pm VE Day, Ed was operated on, had a swell time with sis & Ed., swell kids. VE Day over.

May 9, 1945   Arrived at Ft. Meade, MD. Stayed till June 22. Met Gloria in Washington, DC. Had a swell time at Earle Theatre, Glen Echo, dancing. Also met Mary. Glen Echo had a good roller coaster.

> *[Fire-bombings: Nagoya 5/14 & 5/16; Tokyo 5/23 & 5/25; Yokohama & Osaka 5/26-6/4; Kobe 6/5; Osaka 6/7 & 6/15; Amagaski 6/15... all places John would go]*

[May 10, 1945-June 21, 1945   no dated entry]

> *May 23, 1945 President [23 days] Adm. Karl Dönitz's government ordered dissolved by Eisenhower, with Dönitz's arrest at 10:00am.*

June 22nd – June 26th   Friday till Tuesday night: troop train to Ft. Lawton, Seattle, WA. Scenery in Ft. Lawton was beautiful. Mt. Ranier could be seen from Camp. Had 3 passes in Seattle.

[June 27, 1945-July 1, 1945   no dated entry]

July 2, 1945   Left Ft. Lawton, boarded the S.S. Julian. The band played **"Deep in the Heart of Texas."** The trip up the bay was beautiful. Mountains on both sides. The trip to Honolulu [HA] was very bad. I was seasick the second day out; thought I would die. We slept in a hold five men deep. Ate standing up. We just lay on the deck and read, slept, etc. We all wondered if we were coming back again. Saw whales, sharks, porpoises, flying fish. Horribly homesick.

[July 3, 1945-July 7, 1945   no dated entry]

> *[The Philippines were liberated on 7/5]*

July 10   The Hawaiian Islands came in sight at 11:00am Wed. morning. We docked at 9:00pm that night after running the mine field. Two Jap subs were contacted on the trip but we were very lucky, none of them caused any trouble. We got off the boat Thursday morning. Went to the 13th Regimental Division Depot and stayed in the barracks till Sunday. I went to Waianae for amphibious training. The truck convoy was very long. We were on K-rations for 3 days. We were in 6-man tents then. About ¼ mile from the beach and a small native village. We ate coconuts and saw a lot. We saw a **USO** show of Hawaiian Hula girls dancing in grass skirts under the Pacific moon. It was very beautiful. We made three invasions landings and assaulted the beach three times.

[July 11, 1945-July 17, 1945   no dated entry]

Black Sand beaches of Punaluu, Oahu, Hawaii

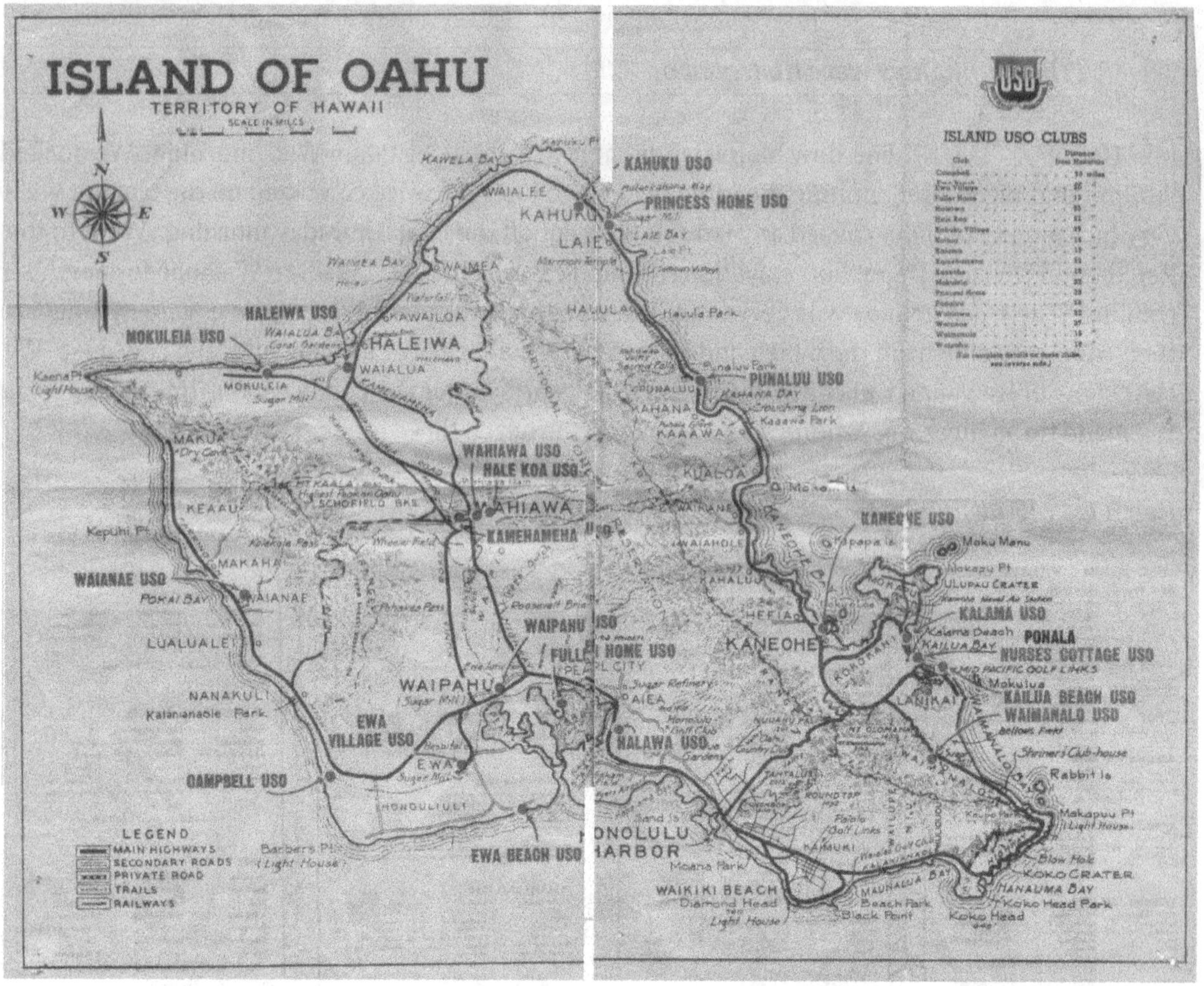

Waianae Army Center, Hawaii

1945-03 John Carriker Jr home from basic training at Ft. Hood

Helemano Army Camp 1946

> *[the first atomic bomb was exploded at a US test facility in New Mexico on 7/16.]*

July 18   Left Wednesday for "Helemano" for weapons training; still in 6-man tents. I studied for the light machine gun, heavy BAR [Browning Automatic Rifle] rifle, bazooka, grenade carbine, all small arms! I studied Japanese weapons. Went to show each night for a week there. Sunday had a wonderful minister from Texas.

[July 19, 1945-July 23, 1945   no dated entry]

> *[The first 'Manhattan Project' bomb [non-nuclear: Component B],*
> *a Pumpkin Bomb, was dropped on July 20,1945.*
> *The Imperial Palace in Tokyo, Japan, was the target but the bomb missed.]*

July 24   We left Tuesday and went to Punaluu on Detached Service. Still in six-man tents. 1st week we put on demonstrations for General Richardson, Paul McNutt, etc. 3rd week, we changed our practice to our Tommy Gun. I went to Honolulu twice. I went through Dole Pineapple Plant. The trip was conducted by a beautiful 18 year old blond girl. Had all the pineapple and juice we could eat or drink free.

[July 25, 1945-August 7, 1945   no dated entry]

> *[The Potsdam Declaration was issued to Japan calling on them to surrender or "face utter destruction." Japan denied the request on July 30th.*
> *Japan was told 8 of its cities would be destroyed if it did not surrender on 7/31.]*

> *The first atomic bomb was dropped on Hiroshima on August 6th.*
> *It was a fission bomb with Uranium 23.*
> *About 160,000 died from the blast {520,000° temperature} and radiation sickness that followed for months.*
> *It is unknown how strong the publicity of the event was at the time.]*

August 8   Wednesday, I had a practice in daytime; went to **USO** about a mile down the road in the morning. I had a night practice, till 12:30[am] we were a surrendering Jap Patrol. The results were very humorous. "Fish" from Spokane and I just walked around amongst them. They did not know what to do.

> *[The second atomic bomb was dropped on Nagasaki on August 9th. It was an Implosion Bomb with Plutonium 240. About 80,000 died from the blast and radiation sickness. It is unknown how strong the publicity of the event was at the time.]*

Punaluu was hit with a tidal wave 9 months after Dad left!

1945-08 Downtown Honolulu

August 9   Thursday, Got a pass to go to Honolulu; went to Waikiki beach also. Was very, very beautiful: the beach, trees, hotel and all. I saw a Hula girl show back in a carnival. It was a good show. I heard **"Green Eyes"** by Jimmy Dorsey, first time since Bat Cave [NC] in 1942. Sure sounded good. Was at **USO** again at night.

August 10   Friday, 1945, at 6 [am] this morning I was awakened by the noise of celebrating Yanks, my buddies. The war was over. I have thanked God for his kindness. We are very lucky. We all winder when we can come home. This morning we hiked up the mountain road. I cleaned an M-1 carbine and M-2 carbine. This afternoon we went down to the **USO**. I had a glass-bottom boat. The tropical fish were beautiful, all colors. The **USO** is George Murphy's summer love. The Palm and coconut trees and blue Pacific are beautiful. We went back to camp and ate chow. Then after chow went back to the **USO**. Hawaiian natives were there and we taught them how to square dance [the girls were good dancers]. I came back to the tent about 10:30pm.

August 11   Saturday, I got up at 6:45am we are all curious when will we go home. We had our picture taken this morning for the Battalion Record. I went to **USO** in the afternoon. I wrote letters and swam in the Pacific. I came back to camp for chow. Went back to **USO**. Walked back and sat on bridge looking out over the ocean. Climbing, feeling good, cause we all know we could someday go home now. At the time, we were to enter combat, 1,300,000 casualties were listed: 300,000 were Navy and Marines and 1,000,000 were Army. 700,000 were Infantry of the Army, so we had all been pretty well scared.

August 12   **[Dad's birthday]** Sunday, Got up about 7:30am. I finally got a pass to go 200 miles to Honolulu. I got to town about 11:30 in the morning. Got my pictures back, also a haircut. Women barbers don't know how to cut hair: 75¢. Rode back to **USO**, most rides in Jeeps. Pali pass with winding road, raw winds, upside-down waterfalls. Saw & heard the colored band called "The Junglers."

Sure were good. Played **"Sentimental Journey."** Very good. Came back to chow, went back to **USO**; wrote letters, then saw show **"Bedside Manner"** and came back to tent.

August 13   Monday, Got up at 6:40am this morning. We train in Air Corp boys today. This morning we taught patrolling to engineers, also this afternoon. It was very hot. We sat down under a makeshift shelter then ran out and showed the correct way to operate. We used Thompson sub-machine guns (Tommy Guns), automatic rifles, carbine and Garand M-1 rifles. Rain and mosquitoes pretty bad. Ate chow, went back to **USO**, saw **"Southern."** I came home to hear that Japs had said OK to our surrender terms. I had a fever again. It was the 3rd time this week already.

August 14   Tuesday, Got up at 7:00am to hear that the Japs, as yet, have not agreed to our terms. I'm getting ready to go to Honolulu. Went through Dole Pineapple plant again with Clarence Engel. At about 2 or 3 in the afternoon the official end of the war was announced. Everyone there in town was delirious with joy. There were parades, traffic jams, paper-throwing and everything. I went into a small church and got on my knees and thanked God for his wonderful kindness. I came home to chow after taking some pictures. I went to the USWO again. Moon was beautifully shining through the trees. Searchlights were playing of love. The sky sure was beautiful.

August 15   Wednesday, Got up at 6:00 this morning. Had one Air Corp class this morning in the cane field. Made Sgt. and officers crawl on their stomachs. At chow at noon. All classes have been discontinued because of the end of the war. Went down to **USO** after chow. Saw picture **"Salome, where she danced."** The most beautiful brunette I've ever seen: Yvonne DeCarlo. For the first time in a long time, I laughed tonight. Came back to tent. Had fever again after going to bed. Felt pretty bad. I am anxious to get home [3800 miles!].

S.S. Cape Johnson

The 98th Infantry at the Wakayama landing in Japan

1945-07 Hawaii, Punnaluu jungle training camp [Oahu] John Carriker Jr

1945-08-05 John Carriker downtown Honolulu. I detached service Pacific Combat Training & Ambushing Instructor

1945-07 John Carriker- Punnaluu, Oahu

August 16   Thursday, Got up at 7:00 am. I ate and took a shower. Slept all morning. Went to **USO** in the afternoon, read and wrote a letter. Walked up the beach and took pictures of a little native boy. I am wondering what they are going to do with us. I had the fever again this afternoon. It usually hits at night. Went to the **USO** and played bongo. Wrote to Ann Louise, Virginia and Dorothy Smith. I saw a 41 Ford maroon convertible. Thought about when I go home to buy my car. I sat by the sign post: the roar of the ocean, the moon over the mountains, Palm Coconut trees; was very impressive.

August 17   Friday, Got up this morning to the nerve-wracking sound of two firecrackers going off under my cot about 6:30am! We start classes again today. I got a pass today. Went to Honolulu and saw a picture show in town **"Unashamed."** Watched them swim at the **USO** pool. Ate dinner in a restaurant in **USO**. All the time wondering when I'll get out of the Army. Came back to camp. Got 4 letters. Went to **USO**. Watched them dance a while, then came back up. Tonight was the 1st time in 6 weeks, since I left the US [mainland] that I've seen a girl I'd like to meet.

August 18   Saturday, Got up at 6:30am and ate hot cakes. Wished I was home. Had a class this morning. I was in the ambush, as a scout. The rain was bad this morning. Saw a beautiful falls up in the mountains. Reminded me of Hickory Nut Falls at Chimney Rock, North Carolina. I ate chow and lay in the tent all afternoon. Went to **USO** after chow and saw a show **"Body Snatchers."** Sat beside a cute girl. We packed up, ready to leave in the morning. The netting cover we have in case we are killed sure doesn't help anybody very much.

August 19   Sunday, Got up at 6:00am, ate, loaded on trucks and drove till noon back to the 13th Regimental Division. We are in barracks again. At noon I got a pass and went to Honolulu. Saw a lot of ships at Pearl Harbor. Saw a jeep turned over in the middle of the road. Went into town, didn't do anything. Went through Schofield Barracks, they have a good swimming pool there. Rode a jeep in, then rode with a Colonel back. Got a letter from Dad. Was issued head net and wound tablets. W.

August 20	Monday, was up at 5:00 for officer's mess, KP. They were served at tables and everything. We ate very good. I never saw anyone bunch of men dirty up so many plates in my life. I had to wash and put them away. Got off at 7:00pm. Got letters from Dad & mom, Ruth, Gloria, Bill O'Neil, Uncle Tommy, Aunt Sue. I was a show **"China Sky"** and **USO** Bob Presley show here tonight. Had a bad fever attack again this afternoon. It comes about every 3-5 days now.

August 21	Tuesday, Woke up with terrible fever and sickness. I felt as though home was a million miles away, there is my luck in the middle of the night. Left the 13th Regimental Division and joined the 98th Infantry Division. I am in a Surveying Section of the Field Artillery; almost was part of the MP's. I am in HQ Battery, 98th Division of 369th Field Artillery. 2nd Battalion is my outfit. I am now due for shoulder patch Blue and Orange Indian Head. Am in the 98th Iroquois Division.

August 22	Wednesday, Got up at 6:30am and ate breakfast. Met my section Sgt. Lida. His name is Jack too. My job requires more jeep driving that anything else. We plot the timeline for the twelve 155-hour trucks. Put it on paper for officers to use. This morning I watched the 12 guns fire out to sea. Boats or planes didn't stop and the planes turned around. We packed boxes this afternoon after supper. Crausby and I showed just on the CKC's and went to see show **"Bette Davis & Olivia de Haviland.** Girl sat in front of us cuddled up to an officer. Made us homesick.

August 23	Thursday, up at 6:20 this morning. Went to Motor Pool at 8:00 to my jeep. I washed it, cleaned it up and stayed with the jeep all day till about 4:00 in the afternoon. Cleaned up and went to the show with Crausby and saw Van Johnson & Esther Williams in **"Thrill of a Romance."** Was a wonderful picture. Sure made Crausby and I want to go home.

August 24	Friday, woke up at 6:30am, ate and went to motor pool at 8:00am. 7 fellows and myself went to Sand Island in Honolulu in a ¾ ton weapons carrier. We drove up over the pass. They (the seven) got seven 2 ½ ton USMC trucks. I got a jeep. I drove the jeep back over the Pali Pass. Brought a bunch of cinnamon cookies and coke. Brought the jeep back here to Ft. Plose. Took 4 shots in the arm. Arm is pretty sore too. I got Typhus, Tetnus, Typhoid and Cholera shots. Took my own jeep and put the top windshield down and packed exhaust pipe and battery up in the air. Fever at 8:00pm and felt as though I were half drawn from shots.

August 25	Saturday, washed my jeep this morning. At 2 in the afternoon put on my suntans [uniform] and reported to the Major in the jeep. He sent me 45 miles through Honolulu to Schofield Barracks for 2 Army nurses and a Lt. Braught. Then went back and took Major to them. At 11:00 I went after them and took them back. 199 miles and got in at 2:30 in the morning. Also saw C.F. Dorsey on the road: beautiful home and law, huge coach, ships and wheel table. Beautiful. We talked a good deal. He knew Uncle Tommy.

August 26	Sunday, went on Honolulu on Pass road with Ledy to the golf course. Got my pictures. In the afternoon I made a seat cover for my jeep. I put a shoulder patch of the 98th on each seat. Really snappy! Made it out of a sheet. I wrote to Ruth Bull, Ruth Hay, Ann, Mary Ann, Mom and Sis.

August 27	Monday, I loaded the trash in the morning. I ate at 10:30am and left at 11:00 in my jeep. I convoyed to Honolulu to put the trucks on a boat. I was behind a slow truck climbing the mountain. Drove through Honolulu; was very noisy with our exhaust in the air. Sat watering trucks till 7:00pm. I ate on the ship and saw Leonard Hohenberger. I came back to the tent about 9:00pm.

August 28	Tuesday, Hauled trash in the afternoon and drove to Billows Field first. Then back and loaded up the jeep and drove Capt. Hyde to the Boat. Saw them load my jeep on the boat. The boat didn't look too bad. I drove back, cleaned up and wrote 10 letters.

1945-08 John Carriker- Governor's Palace Grounds, Honolulu

August 29		Wednesday, worked in the PX today. Hauled coke bottles and worked behind the counter dishing out orange juice. General came in and bought orange juice. He made a remark that he didn't like it. I said "It's G7, sir." Went to the show **"Tin Pan Alley."**

August 30		Thursday, Hauled huge floors to the dump in the morning. Lot of planes thrown away. I drove to Schofield in the afternoon. A trailer on my jeep was full of equipment to turn in. I ate at the PX and drove back through Honolulu the same way. I went to Broadway **USO** and saw **"Dear Ruth"** with real actors and it was very good.

August 31		Friday, Just lay around all morning and haven't done a thing. Everything is loaded on the boats and there is nothing left to do. We went to the **USO** (Railua) to swim. It sure was beautiful.

September 1		Saturday, Just swam again. We are only marking time till we get on the boat on Wednesday.

September 2		Sunday, I went to church this morning and went swimming again.

> *[The documents to officially end the war were signed on this day aboard the USS Missouri in Tokyo Bay.]*

September 3		Monday, K.P. Today. Oh Misery! Saw **"Our Vines Have Tender Grapes"** and **"Johnny Angel,"** both very excellent.

1945-07 John Carriker Jr, Oahu [no assignment]

1945-08 Me in Honolulu

September 4		Tuesday, Went to Honolulu and bought ribbons, stripes, haircut and patches. Saw Shirley Temple in **"Kiss and Tell"** and it was very, very good. Also saw **"Mob Hill."** It was good too. They are at the open theatre.

September 5		Wednesday, A lot of the fellows are getting on the boat today. I guess we will get on tomorrow. I dread this trip. They say we will be 3 weeks getting there. I won't get any more mail for a long while. I sure miss it. I keep wondering about my future wife. I think of her night and day, wondering who she will be. Saw **"Capt. Kidd"** and **"Within These Walls."** They say it will be a 17 day boat ride. We expect to go by Saipan.

September 6		Thursday, We think we are going to Osaka on the main island of Japan (Honshu). Sometime I feel as though I will go crazy just dreaming. If it wasn't for Mom & Dad and Don, I would be insane already. We ate sandwiches etc., waited around all day. I bought some magazines at the Naval Base. I saw a Negro ball game while waiting on the trucks. The ride through Honolulu was ok- a drunk sailor caused a little trouble but our Colonel driver stopped that. Got on the boat about 9:30pm. Didn't look forward to the trip at all.

September 7		Friday, I got up and ate. We left Hickam Field where the boat was docked about noon. Began getting sick around supper time. I couldn't eat supper and went back to my bunk (top one out of five) and lay there one hour. I have never been sicker in my life. I felt as though I were dying. I am not feeling too well for about four months now. I keep having sick spells. These come and go. About I would get a boat. I slept on deck all night- a blanket under me and over me. An iron floor is not too soft.

September 8		Saturday, Got up and ate one apple. I feel plenty weak. I read some. I sat in the truck; sat under the jeep when it rains. I read with Bud Hare, a new friend of mine from Virginia. We talk a lot and are very, very tired. We all want to go home so bad. There are around 30 ships in our convoy. I ate a little more dinner and supper. I am nursing a terrific headache. I am in a bad fix mentally. I would give anything to get back home. I keep wondering about my girl. I wonder who she will be. There is a band that is going to play music. It helps a lot. It also makes us awfully homesick. The band played **"It Had to be You," "A Dream," "My Dreams are Getting Better," "Candy"** and **"All the Time."** We are to go to Saipan first (11 day trip) them 9 more days to Japan.

September 9		Sunday, Trusting in God surely does help tremendously. I hope I will make a good minister like Daddy. If only the folks in the US could realize the price that Freedom does cost. We had church service on one of the hatches. I sat in the front seat of a big truck, tied on deck and listened. It was a nice service. We were eager to hear a good service. It was so strange a setting for church. The ship machinery, landing boats, jeeps, trucks were tied everywhere. But we know God was there. Slept on the hood of one of the landing boats.

September 10		Monday, I got up and ate. I was on Guard today. My post was at the stairway. I was on 2 hours and off 4 hours as usual. I keep thinking of home. I remember Guard Duty at the camps. The girls giving me candy, etc., while walking my post at Ft. Meade. The cold at Ft. Sam Houston, the prisoners. The milk chauffeur and I drank at Ft. Hood. You have a lot of time to think. The band plays every night. We are fortunate to have the band on our ship. Daydreaming a lot about going home.

September 11		Tuesday, I ate three meals and reading was about all. Each day is the same aboard ship. Today ended at noon as we crossed the International Date Line.

> *[Japanese General Tojo attempted suicide by shooting himself in the stomach, but he survived.]*

[above] bombed oil refinery near Tokyo; [below] bombed power plant in Ube

September 12   Wednesday, we crossed the Date Line at noon so today started at noon. I sat around and read, was all. After supper each night the Division band plays and we all gather round. Some of the songs make us really homesick.

September 13   Thursday, I slept on the hood of a landing craft. It is getting hotter as we near Saipan. We should get there Tuesday night the 18th [5 days]. The band played **"I Should Care"** and **"I Never Smile Again."** Both really made me want to be home again. I'd give every cent I have just to look at a good American girl.

September 14   Friday, I wrote a few letters. It is much hotter. The fever hasn't bothered me for about 6 days; maybe it is the salt air. The band played after supper. It nice to hear some good music.

September 15   Saturday, It was just a normal day. Read and wrote a few letters. I ate and also saw the picture **"A Song to Remember."** The band was very good. They played Glenn Miller's theme song and dedicated it to him [missing in flight 12/15/1944]. The effect on the fellows was very surprising and recurrent.

September 16   Sunday, Church was held in the evening. I became familiar with SMCI. The moon was bright and the dark was fast setting in and the song **"Day is Dying in the West."** It was very impressive.

September 17   Monday, I just read and ate all day. Not feeling good at all.

September 18   Tuesday, I have Class this morning and have a terrific headache. Went on sick call about lungs and was told to wait till we hit Japan. Band played again tonight and really helped a lot.

September 19   Wednesday, about 3:00am it rained so and I was sleeping on deck I had to get up. So I went down and took a shower and shaved and came back up. Then I could see Tinian. [south of Saipan] The lights were on. About noon we docked off Saipan. The picture **"Keys of the Kingdom"** was the show. The land sure looked good after so much water.

September 20   Thursday, This morning we went over to another ship and refueled. We just lay around all say. I bought a Sterncrest pipe [no longer has it] at the ships service store. I like it a lot. **"Practically Yours"** was the picture.

September 21   Friday. We got up this morning and went to shore in landing boats. We went in swimming about 3 miles down the road. There was all sort of shells, bullets, tanks, boats wrecked and rusted lay around. Saw quite a few Jap POW's. We came back to the ship about 1:00pm. We had our first mail in 21 days. It was sure swell to get letters again. I got mail from Ruth Hay, Mary Ann, Ann Louise, Barbara June, Mom, Dad, Aunt Clarine, Sis & Ed (14 letters). I sure wish I could go see Rich. This island is about 10 miles from where we are docked. We saw the picture **"Dragon Seed."**

September 22   Saturday, We left Saipan early this morning at 3:00 or 4:00. I wrote letters to everyone: Mom, Dad, Don, Mary Ann, Ruth, Ann, Barbara Poolent, Sis & Ed, Uncle Cecil and Aunt Clarine. We expect to hit Japan the 27th of September. We had ice cream today.

September 23   Sunday, I went to church this morning. It was another impressive service on the Deck. Nothing much doing. I felt quite sick. The sea was very rough. I slept on deck under the landing boat.

September 24   Monday, We did nothing again today. I bought a coke & 2 ice creams. It cost me a dollar. I had to bribe a sailor. I was on Guard Duty again.

September 25   Tuesday, We turned in our money today. We were told our instructions for landing, etc. We are all very excited to see what Japan is like. I read an excellent book **"Bermuda Calling."** It sure was a good one. We expect to see land tomorrow (Japan).

May 1945- Tokyo- Saiban- Ichigawa

May 1945- Bombed out Yokohama and harbor

September 26   Wednesday, We expected to see land today, but we didn't. It is getting cooler as we go north. There isn't much of importance about today. Just wish I were home as usual. The band played tonight again.

September 27   Thursday, There are close to 200 ships not moving in the harbor, if not 300. It is raining and cold out. Quite different from our tropical climate. They have been unloading the ships all day. As yet (3:00pm), we aren't off the boat and may stay on till tomorrow. We are at Wakayama and expect to go to Osaka as soon as we get off the ship. Read **"Earth and High Heaven"** today (about a Jewish Canadian). It is 7:00pm and am going to the shop. It is cold and very rainy out (very distressing). It was hard on our nerves.

September 28, 1945   Friday, I think we will get off today. We got off the boat at 9:00 this morning. I hit the beach at 9:33am. We ate dinner, "C" rations. There are little Japanese all around lugging. It was pitiful to see the way these people live. Just like natives. It was worse than any slum in the U.S. We hiked 6 miles to the train and went to Osaka. We got off and marched to an airfield and bivouacked on the landing strips. The Japanese were all standing and staring as we walked through the alleys. My jeep went off [the boat] in 4½' of water, so it is not running.

September 29   Saturday, Got up and ate my "C" rations. I went over to the airplanes (Jap) and got a few souvenirs: a briefcase and a seat and a few dials [a compass in a box]. American planes are on the airfield also: B-17 (General Stillwell's plane), C-47's, P-51's. Williams & I pitched our pup tents and are in it now. We don't know what to expect. We surveyed the area and are in a company area now.

September 30   Sunday, We went down to the beach and picked up more supplies. We went to the beach in a truck convoy: 17 trucks and 2 jeeps. It was very dusty and dirty. All the people came out and waved and some saluted us. They were all very friendly, but nothing but slaves. The villages were very small. A truck could just barely go down the streets with about 3" clearance. We saw the bombed out area of Osaka and Wakayama. It surely was destroyed.

October 1   Monday, I dug latrines. It was very hard. I sure hate digging! That is about all I did.

October 2   Tuesday, We built houses and wash racks. In the afternoon we went after water. We took 5 hours to get it. It took so long waiting in line. While waiting we tried trading with the people. The water point was right in the middle of the street. I tried to talk to them and made a little headway. I bought some chop sticks for 15 Sen. It was about 1¢ in American money.

October 3   Wednesday, Wednesday, we dug today one 15'x5'x4' hole and one 8'x8'x8' hole. It sure is rough. We first made new tent today. It is raining today. I hope we can keep dry tonight. This sure is a ----- of a way for the conquering Army to live. Everyone is disgusted.

October 4   Thursday, today it still is pouring down rain. Everything is under water 5" deep. We got 4 big tents and cots so we will keep up out of the water. We went to the warehouse and unloaded food. We ate cans of fruit, cookies, etc. I got in about 10:00pm.

October 5   Friday, I got up cold and put on soaking wet cold clothes. It was very uncomfortable and still pouring down rain. The 391st is in one foot of water. Everyone is miserable. We rode around and pitched 2 more big tents.

October 6   Saturday, we didn't do much today. I helped Wade clean the engine in his ¾ ton weapons carrier in the morning. We didn't do much in the afternoon either. I came in and went to sleep early. Still, there is no mail. I got paid 75 yen for the $3 I turned in on the SS Cape Johnson.

1945-05-29 B-29s in action over Yokohama

1945-05-29 Yokohama bombing

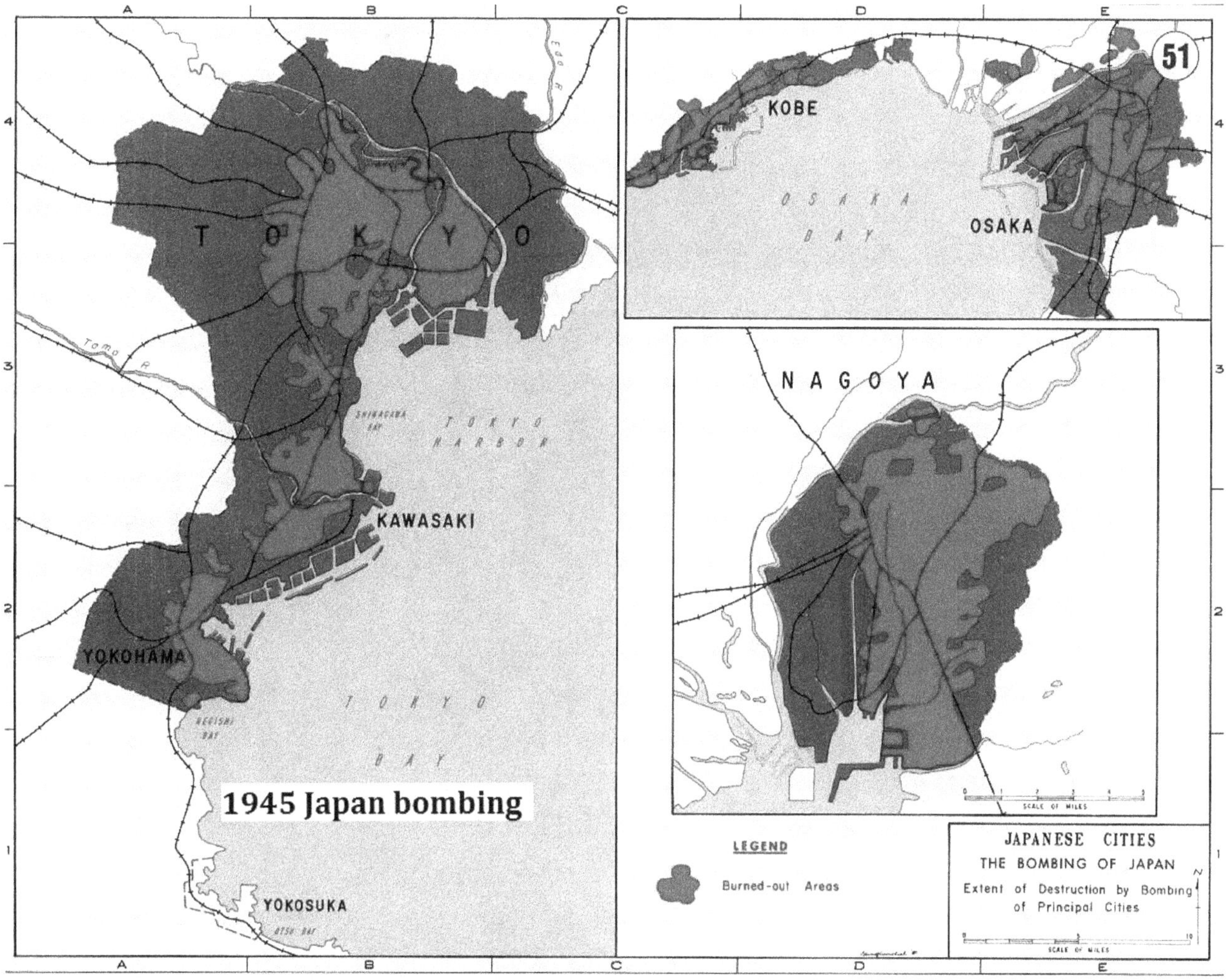

1945 Japan bombing

1945-07 Scuttled aircraft carrier in Tokyo Bay

1945-07 Yokohama after bombing

1945-07 temporary huts in Yokohama after bombing

October 7   Sunday, we got up this morning and put a Japanese motorcycle together. Ruderick did it. I went to church, which was held on the runway under the wing of a C-47. It was a good sermon. This afternoon we went on a trip through Osaka. It sure was burned and bombed out. It looked just like a junk pile. The Japanese pay 20 yen ($1.20) for one package of cigarettes. The same for comb and soap. The girls try to give themselves away for a few cigarettes. It sure it pitiful… these people are just slaves.

October 8   Monday, today I went to have an x-ray taken and they said return tomorrow. They told us about our new camp today. I got my jeep today and my new one. Was it ever dirty! I cleaned it up but someone stole the top. It is raining again.

October 9   Tuesday, today it is still raining. We got up and some of the fellows went to the new camp. I and Devine were on unloading detail down at the warehouse. We ate a lot of fruit. I came back to the battery area and it is still raining. Still no mail. I sure wish the mail would get here. I am not feeling too good tonight. I am running a fever again. I sure wish I could go home.

October 10   Wednesday, Devine and I were on KP today. We just scrubbed pots and pans and ate all day. They said a gale was coming about 6:30pm so we fastened all our tents down better. It wasn't so bad though. I think it blew over mostly. Still no mail. I just daydream about going home most of the time. My jeep is up at the new area at Nara. I guess we go up in a couple of days.

October 11   Thursday, I cleaned my knife and carbine for an inspection this morning. I sat around most of the morning. The Japs do a good bit of the work. I didn't do much till after supper. We went to the warehouse and unloaded trucks again. We ate pineapple, apricots, peaches and everything. Got in about 1:00am.

October 12   Friday, I slept all morning. We got our first letters. I got 6 letters: 4 from Mom & Dad, 1 from Ann and 1 from Gloria. I went on Guard Duty at 4:30 in the afternoon. We were 2nd General Order. I bought a kimono and socks. Boy was it cold last night on Guard [Duty].

October 13   Saturday, It was freezing cold on Guard this morning, 3-5am. We built a fire and kept warm. 9-11am I was warm. I talked to a policeman for a while. I went on Guard Duty again at 3pm and was not released until 6pm. Sure was cold. I came into chow and had 17 letters. It sure is swell to get mail. I heard that Laura Belle died. I sure will miss her.

October 14   Sunday, I got up and took all of the tents down and got into the trucks and came up to Nara, Japan to our barracks. It is better than mud and tents. I got about 10 more letters and heard from June in a note. I sure am homesick.

October 15   Monday, Today we got up and ate then I took my jeep and reported to Maj. Zimmer and took him to a school, then into Nara to some stores, then to the Nara Prefecture (county, I guess) Building. In the afternoon we looked till we found a lumber yard. We went all over Nara and saw a beautiful park. These people surely are primitive. They all walk all over the street. I got paid 844.20 Yen. It sure is a big pile of money!

October 16   Tuesday, This morning I cleaned up my jeep. After dinner I reported to Maj. Zimmer. After a long wait (letter to Burke) we went to town and had a talk with the Colonel on the way. We went to the Prefecture Office. While waiting I wrote to Jim. Many Japs gathered around to stare at my strange writing. Some of them (2) spoke English. They were amazed at my pay and American and My jeep. We came back and ate and I made a top letter. I sewed on some stripes!

The remnants of the Japanese Air Force in 1946 at Taisho Airfield

1945-08 Osaka

October 17		Wednesday, Today we went for lumber again. In the afternoon, Major Zimmer & I & an interpreter went about 14 miles from Nara to a small town where Americans had not yet been. Soon after I stopped the usual group gathered around my jeep. There were more than 50-75 people all very curious. The Japanese are immensely surprised at our 'gentlemen dress.' They expected [us to be] beast as they are. I can't figure the Japanese out. I went back after a truck which ran out of gas. On the way back I passed the "cat house" district. It certainly is a shame.

October 18		Thursday, I got up early and went to Taisho airfield. Maj. Zimmer was reporting to a Colonel and found that he is to inspect factories to see if Division should place Guards at them and make sure there are no war activities. We inspected 2 factories today and drove back to Nara. I prepared for the trip the next morning. I guess I'll be gone about a month. It should prove interesting.

October 19		Friday, We loaded up our things and left Nara early and came to Taisho airfield again. For the present I am with Division Headquarters Company. We drove to a factory this morning and came to an area of Osaka which was flooded. My jeep almost got drowned out. We ate uptown in Osaka. I ate at the Red Cross building close to Club Kabuki and Club International. In the afternoon we went to a large tractor plant and then back to Taisho. I set up my bunk, checked my jeep and went to bed.

October 20		Saturday, I got up at 6 o'clock, drew my cigarettes, ate and at 8 o'clock reported to Maj. Zimmer. We went to a factory in Osaka where I got a Jap first aid load. There is a Major & two Lieutenants, an interpreter and two jeeps and drivers today. I bought a cigarette case for 5¢ and a silver tie clasp. We went up town to eat. I bought 3 small wrist compasses for 7 Yen. In the afternoon we went to a battery factory and also we went to another one where I washed the jeep. I saw a pretty girl at the battery plant. She showed me to the "Benjo" [便所, a toilet] and gave me some tea. They all gave up tea. I saw my first show in 4 weeks; a **USO** show on sing your way home.

October 21		Sunday, We got up and went to a factory close to the airfield. At about 10:30am we started for Nara. I got here in time to eat. I picked up some mail which was sure appreciated and just sat around in the afternoon. At 8 o'clock I went after the Major and Colonel and took them to the Nara Hotel. I waited for the Colonel till 11 o'clock and then went back to the barracks.

October 22		Monday, I got up at 5:30 this morning. I went to the Nara Hotel after Maj. Zimmer. We drove to Osaka and inspected a couple of plants. I got a fan, clock and some other stuff. I ate dinner uptown at the Red Cross. We took in a couple more factories and saw a little boy that reminded me of June. I saw **Danny Kaye & Leo "Lippy" Durocher** [an American profession baseball player] at the Kitano theatre uptown [for a live performance]. It sure was good.

October 23		Tuesday, I got up and went after the Major and inspected a gun factory. We went to another factory and then uptown to dinner. In the afternoon we took in some more plants and then went home to chow. I saw the show ***"Ten Cents a Dance"*** [Barbara Stanwyck] in the barracks.

October 24		Wednesday, We inspected another plant and looked for another one for quite a while. Finally gave up. We then took in another plant. We ate uptown as usual. I bought a very nice case for my camera. Wednesday night we drove up to Nara. I stayed there at the barracks all night. I took Major Zimmer to the Nara Hotel and while there I took a bath. I got to camp around 11 o'clock [pm]. It surely is cold.

October 25		Thursday, I got up at 5:30am and ate and went into Nara to the Nara Hotel and picked up Major Zimmer and the Lieutenant and drove to Osaka. We inspected more factories and I washed and oil my jeep. We ate uptown and after dinner took in some more plants. I got some bumper Guards and whetstones at that one. After we got back, I saw the show ***"Don Juan Quilligan** [1945]." It sure was good. William Bendix [Joan Blondell, Phil Silvers] played in it.

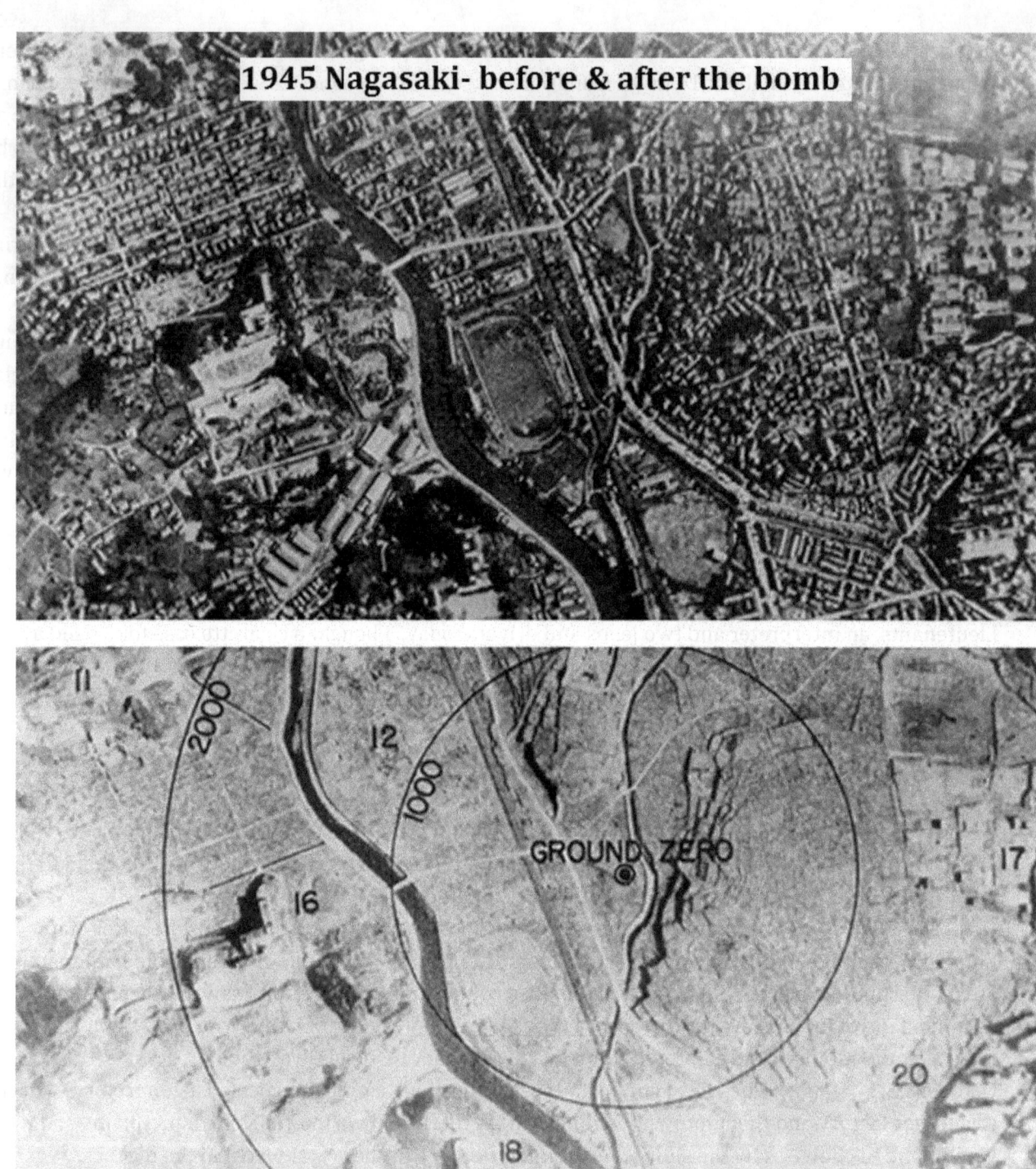

October 26	Friday, I got up and picked up Major Zimmer, a Lieutenant & interpreter and drove to the other side of Osaka where we inspected a huge plant. We ate uptown again and in the afternoon we went to a place in Sakai, about 17 miles and there they gave me a potato to eat. We then went back to the Taisho Airfield and I greased the jeep and went to bed.

October 27	Saturday, I got up at 6am and went to a factory out in the end of Osaka and through it. I ate uptown and bought a black cigarette box for 120 Yen, which is $8 in American money. We then went way out to a diamond factory. These wooden shoes and baggy pants they wear. Ugh!! We drove up to Nara and it sure is a rough road.

October 28	Sunday, I went to Nara to church this morning. I also bought some fans and chop sticks. Our chapel is across from the train station. In the afternoon the Major and Interpreter and I went about 14 miles up in the hills to an old pottery maker. We had tea and he took us in his house. Off came our shoes and we squatted and ate chestnuts and drank tea. He showed us his process for making pottery. It surely is primitive. He gets the correct heat by smelling the fire. He made a vase while were there and gave me a plate and plaque and a painting.

October 29	Monday, I pulled four wheels on the jeep and repacked them [with grease]. I went on Guard at 3:00 in the afternoon. I was getting a 6000 mile checkup on the jeep. Guard [Duty] wasn't bad. We had Jap overcoats. I saw Joan Leslie in *"Cinderella Jones."*

October 30	Tuesday, Guard [Duty], didn't do much. I fixed a tire for my jeep and painted the dashboard and fooled around in Guard [Duty]. I saw the picture *"Weekend Pass"* [Noah Berry, Jr. and Martha O'Driscoll].

October 31	Wednesday, I was on Stand-By with the jeep today. I went to Nara 6 times and drove to a gravel pit. The Lieutenant bought a Kimono. I got off at 8:30pm.

November 1	Thursday, Stand-By again this morning. I went to Nara 3 times. In the afternoon I was on KP Duty with Gagloid. I got paid 743 Yen.

November 2	Friday, I didn't do much and hauled cement all day. At night, Andy & I went to a Geisha house and got us a girl. Boy, were they a scream. We talked and they danced. They were strange and really cute. Mine had a name like June's.

November 3	Saturday, I was on standby for Maj. Lewis today. The Colonel used my jeep. Late in the afternoon we went to Nara. I saw Katsu Ha (Geisha girl). She sure was surprised to see me in my jeep.

November 4	Sunday, I drove Lt. Hoffman to church in the morning. I ate chow and just sat around in the afternoon and wrote letters. Sunday night I took Lt. Hoffman and Lt. Hicks to town and they let me have the jeep from 6:30 to 10:00pm. I went over to the Geisha house and got Andy and Katuka and took them for a ride. That poor little girl was scared to death, but she really loved it. She said "Jeep-oo nice-oo. Speed-oo?" So I took off at about 30 mph. She was screaming and hollering; just scared silly. She really liked it though. She is a beautiful girl. She says "Jonny nice-oo."

November 5	Monday, I took Maj. Zimmer & Lt. Johnston to Osaka. We are still inspecting factories. I did quite a bit of driving. I bought 2 Jap opium pipes and went to the show. At the Kitano Theatre. I saw Humphrey Bogart and Lauren Bacall in *"The Big Sleep."* It was very good.

November 6	Tuesday, I drove out to the bay and saw a nice Packard convertible half under water. I got nails in 3 of my tires.

November 7	Wednesday, I went out to the bay again and got a flat. I had to use my dictionary to borrow a jack from the Japanese. I went to a show and sat beside a girl that looked like Gene Tierney. I took a little boy to the show.

1945-08 Surrender of Yamashita & Tojo

Bombing Raids in Japan: March 9 - June 15, 1945

Raid #	Date	Cities	B-29's	Lost	Damaged	Bombs	Deaths	Buildings lost	Area[sq. mi.]	Notes
1	1945/03/09	Tokyo #1	334	14	40	1700 tons incen.	100,000	167,171	15.8	3 hour raid; total d/bdg
2	1945/03/11	Nagoya #1	313	1	20	[1565 tons]	0	0	2	
3	1945/03/13	Osaka #1	274	2	13	[1370 tons]	4,666	134,944	8	3 hour raid
4	1945/03/16	Kobe	[250]			[1250 tons]	8,841	65,961	3	Japanese fighters
5	1945/03/19	Nagoya #2	[250]			[1250 tons]	0	0	3	
6	1945/04/07	Tokyo #2	[250]			[1250 tons]	0	0	11.4	
7	1945/04/15	Tokyo #3				[1500 tons]	0	102,317	6	
7	1945/04/15	Kawasaki	303	12		[2000 tons]	0	31,603	3.6	
7	1945/04/15	Yokohama #1				[2000 tons]	0	15,000	1.5	
8	1945/05/14	Nagoya #3	471	10		2515 tons incen.	0	0	3.15	18 Japanese fighters lost
9	1945/05/16	Nagoya #4	457			3609 tons	3,869	113,460	3.82	
10	1945/05/23	Tokyo #4	520			[4100 tons]	0	0	5.3	
11	1945/05/25	Tokyo #5	502			[3000 tons]	0	0	16.8	[6 raids equalled 56.3 sq. mi.]
12	1945/05/26-6/4	Yokohama #2	517			[4085 tons]	0		6.9	150 Zekes/ P-51's destroyed 49
13	1945/05/26-6/4	Osaka #2	[400]			[2400 tons]	0		3.15	
14	1945/06/05	Kobe #2	530			[2400 tons]	0	51,399	4.35	
15	1945/06/07	Osaka #3	[400]			[2400 tons]	0	1000 ind.	2.21	
16	1945/06/15	Osaka #4	500			[3500 tons]	0		1.9	
17	1945/06/15	Amagasaki				x	0	severe	0.6	
		TOTALS	6960	136		41,592 tons	333,000 deaths			[Japan said on 7/2 that over 5,000,000 were killed and wounded in the American fire bombings.]
	1945/08/06	Hiroshima	1/7	0		141 lbs U-235/ 4.85 tons 16,000 tons of force	day 1: 80,000; day 2-120: +80,000 of 350,000 residents * 31 **not** dropped * or used			
	1945/08/09	Nagasaki	1/6	0		14 lbs Pl / 5.15 tons 21,000 tons of force	day 1: 40,000; day 2-120: +40,000 of 263,000 people [249,000+12,500 Koreans+600 Chinese+400 Allied POWs * 119 **not** dropped * or used			

Wakayama beach landing

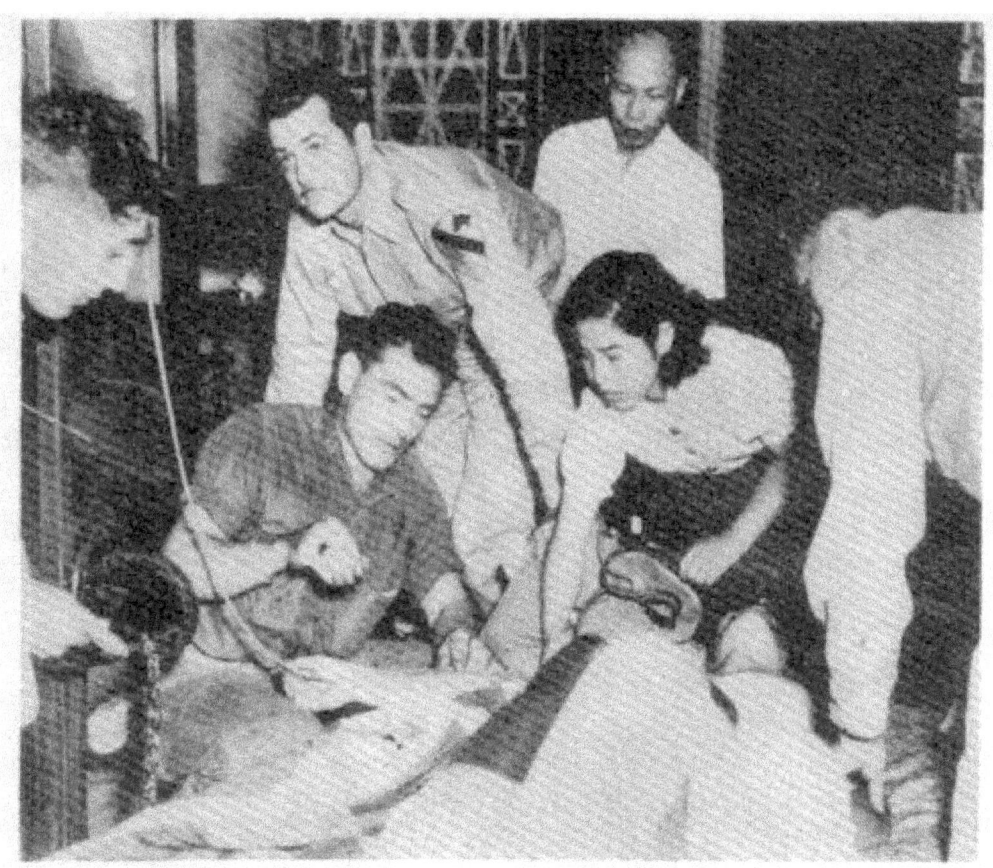
The above picture shows members of the First Cavalry with Japanese Nurse and attendant as they administer blood plasma to Tojo after shooting himself, on the right is Capt. William Trout, of the C. I. C.

**1945-09 attempted suicide- Tojo
September 11, 1945**

Capt. William Trout [left]

1945-10 An office girl of ours of the factories we inspected in front of shrine, Osaka

November 8	Thursday, we inspected more plants. We drove to town about 15 miles away this morning. In the afternoon we got a couple more plants. At night a fellow and I went to see **"Wilson."** It was a pretty good show. We first road the subway to the Umeda Station and got a shoe shine for 1 Yen, about 6¢. I flirted with the gals and went to the show. I sure am glad June wrote and sent her pictures. I think an awful lot of June. I think she is pretty darn nice as well as beautiful. I hope to see her when I get home. I'm sure ready to go home. I don't know whether I'll get to go with the drive next spring or not. I sure hope so.

November 9	Friday, I am still out looking at factories. At night I went with another fellow on the subway to see the Yashinara District. It sure was a mess out there.

November 10	Saturday, we went out this morning and looked over some more plants. In the afternoon we got one plant and them at 3 o'clock Major Zimmer and I started for Nara. I saw a jeep skid on some oil and turn around and then turn over. It was the driver and a Captain in it. I just missed hitting a Jap that walked from behind a truck. Driving is hard here in Japan and in a Jeep there is always that chance of turning over and that is no good with me.

November 11	Sunday, I got up and ate and am going to go to Church this morning. I sure an homesick. I went to church and took communion. In the afternoon Gummer Lindel and I went in a Richshaw through Nara Park. We saw the huge 55' Buddha and had our picture taken.

November 12	Monday, I went back to Osaka. Maj. Zimmer let me use the jeep and goof around and at night went to Kitano Theatre and saw Esther Williams and Van Johnson in **"Thrill of a Romance."** It was very good.

November 13	Tuesday, I had the Jeep all morning. I got two lights, horn, etc. I brought Maj. Zimmer back. We saw a Jeep turn over in Osaka. Saw the picture **"Her Highness and Bellboy"** with Heddy Lamour and June Allyson. It was sweet.

November 14	Wednesday, I got up and it was raining all morning. I drove to Osaka in the afternoon and ate chow and wrote letters. I am expecting some replacements in tonight. I go on Guard [Duty] tomorrow morning.

November 15	Thursday, I was on Guard [Duty] all day at the Ammunition Dump. It is still cold and raining.

November 16	Friday, I took Lt. Hoffman to town this morning and also in the afternoon. I hauled dirt in a weapons carrier and then took a fellow to Division Artillery in my Jeep.

November 17	Saturday, All of us fell out dressed in Kakis. We paraded and dedicated the camp to Lt. Mardin. General Loome was here. Afterward, he came to our barracks. I never put a tie on so fast in my life. I had KP all afternoon.

November 18	Sunday, I went to church this morning and was on Guard [Duty] in the afternoon.

November 19	Monday, I was on Guard [Duty] till about 5 o'clock. I was in the woods at the ammo dump. It sure was cold at night. I built a fire to keep warm.

November 20	Tuesday, I drove a ¾ ton truck carrying fellows back and forth to school in Nara all day. It sure is hard to drive one of those trucks.

November 21	Wednesday, I was on MP Duty patrolling in my Jeep with a two-way radio. The Japs just couldn't understand [what] I was telling [them] and then over the speaker comes the "MP's" at the "Ha." The Japs were really baffled. A GI and a girl and Jap were murdered and thrown in the river last night. They don't know who did it. It is raining all the time.

October 1945 in my Jeep in front of the Colonel's house at Camp Mardin at Nara, Japan

1945 Japanese subs at Maizuru Naval Base + one U-boat for training [rt]

1945-10 John Carriker Jr- Nara, Japan

1945-10 Osaka, Dad's jeep & a requisitioned Datsun auto

1945-11 John Carriker Jr Ricshaw in Nara, Japan

November 22	Thursday, THANKSGIVING I went and had my picture taken with Clyde J. Caskey. I went to church and had turkey and Gasoline for dinner. I took some Jap workers back to Nara this afternoon. I'm on Stand-By and Guard [Duty] tomorrow.

November 23	Friday, I drove the ¾ ton truck to 923rd Field Artillery school and took the fellows in and brought them back. I took two shots at noon and went on Guard [Duty]. I ate and stood post by the Motor Park. Is sure is cold; only about 3-4⁰ in the morning.

November 24	Saturday, I was on Guard [Duty] all day. At 6 o'clock I took Capt. Handell and a couple of other officers to a party at the Nara Hotel. Generals and 5 nurses were there. I went to the Geisha House for about an hour to see Kataki. Two Japs were murdered and MP's patrolled with us to look for knives. He was drunk and firing his rifle.

November 25	Sunday, I went to church in Nara. It sure was a good sermon on us as apostles. I drove to Division Artillery after chow and wrote letters in the afternoon.

November 26	Monday, I drove to Osaka today and it sure was raining hard. I went into the Red Cross building and had coffee. It was a nice place.

November 27	Tuesday [nothing]

November 28	Wednesday, I went on Sick Call with my pain in my stomach. They sent me to the hospital and I had a chest x-ray. I was ok, I guess. I sure was feeling rough.

November 29	Thursday, I was on Sick Call, feeling just dead. They didn't do a thing for me except to tell me to come back if I get worse. I washed the Jeep all afternoon.

November 30	Friday, A big command inspection is on Saturday. We are working hard (very hard). I went on Guard [Duty] in the afternoon. I had to be released because of my side. It sure has been paining me this week. These Army medics don't do a thing except tell me it's my constipation. I think I'm going to go crazy.

December 3	Monday, I drove and was on Stand-by for the 923rd Field Artillery. Today I went to Yagi after laundry about 5:30 in the afternoon. I thought of Mom, Dad and Don. I went to sleep and I guess for the first time in years, I wept.

December 4	Tuesday, I drove to Osaka in the rain and cold, over the Mountain Road, in by the 390th Infantry. I went to the Red Cross for coffee and doughnuts. They have a swell place.

December 5	Wednesday, I went on Guard [Duty] in the afternoon and walked around Officers' Quarters for my part.

December 6	Thursday, I was on Guard [Duty].

December 7	Friday, I drove for Capt. Hyde at Division Artillery all day and got a Jap Coat. In the afternoon I got back and ate chow and took a Jeep out for a riot squad and patrolled the streets till 6 in the morning. We had Grease Guns (Tommy Guns) and Carbines. Command Control was afraid of a riot.

December 8	Saturday, I drove to Osaka this morning and sat around all afternoon. I saw Snyder listening to a record of his little girl and wife and tears came to his eyes. It was a heart-warming night.

December 9	Sunday, I drove for the MP's all day. I started at 7 o'clock and quit at 1 o'clock Monday morning. There was a lot of driving. There was a rape case while I was on Duty.

December 10	Monday I was **Promoted to Cpl. Tech. 5th Grade**. This morning I drove to Division Artillery airfield. I got a wiper motor and some other motors for the motor shop. I went on Guard [Duty] at 3:30 in the afternoon. It sure was cold all night.

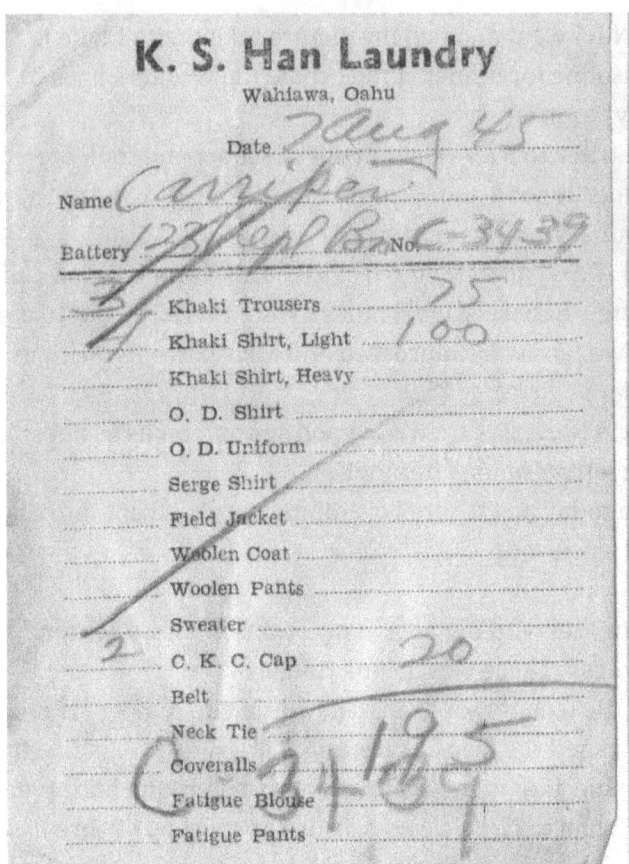

A Laundry Ticket for Dad **War Crimes Trial information card [later]**

1945 Japanese tankettes- 3 tonners with 16.5mm guns

December 11   Tuesday, I was on Guard [Duty] all day. I drove to town with Lt. Hoffman after supper and about froze to death! I got 3 packages- two from Sis & Ed and 1 from Mary Ann.

December 12   Wednesday, I was on KP all day; it was very uninteresting. I was promoted to Cpl. Technician 5th Grade on the 10th.

December 13   Thursday, I went to Osaka to the train station and unloaded freight cars of Chinese coins and gave 5 Japs 5 cigarettes and they worked all afternoon for me.

December 14   Friday, I changed the oil in my Jeep in the morning, drove to Division Artillery and went on Guard [Duty] in the afternoon. We got our mattresses today.

December 15   Saturday, I was on Guard [Duty] all day. There was nothing of interest and quite cold.

December 16   Sunday, I got up about 8 o'clock and ate. At about 10 o'clock I drove Maj. Zimmer to Division Artillery and came back. In the afternoon I drove Maj. Zimmer and Maj. Simon to Nara where they looked around. I saw a Japanese circus which was really an experience.

December 17   Monday, I drove to Division Artillery airfield this morning at 7 o'clock and returned at 9 o'clock and them to Osaka to pick up Capt. Handell. I was told I was to drive for the Provost Marshall up at Tsu. Afterward, I went on Guard [Duty].

December 18   Tuesday, I drove for the MP's from 7 in the morning till midnight. It was an interesting time. This was on Monday and Tuesday.

December 19   Wednesday, I was on Guard [Duty] all day. It is very cold. I like to froze last night. I thought of Mary Ann quite a bit and how nice she would look to me in a sweater right now. It would me feel warm just to see her warm.

December 20   Thursday, Today I didn't do much of anything, but loafed around the garage. I drove Lt. Hoffman to town at night.

December 21   Friday, I was on KP [Duty] all day; nothing of any interest except a red crowned girl ate dinner at the mess hall. She sure did look swell. I saw **"Along Came Jones"** at night. [Gary Cooper & Loretta Young].

December 22   Saturday, Today I hauled cement all morning and in the afternoon. I drove Maj. Simon to Tanbanbi. Then at night I drove Lt. Hicks to see the Christmas lights of Division Artillery.

December 23   Sunday, I went to church this morning and talked to the Red Cross girls and heard a good sermon on the Shepherds hearing of Christ's birth.

December 24   Monday, I went to see Christmas decorations with a Major & General. Then at night I went to an 11 o'clock church service at the chapel. Two Red Cross girls were there. It sure was a nice service.

December 25   Tuesday, Christmas 1945, there was never such a lonely day that should have been otherwise. I drove Capt. Handell to Mass and Sgt. Meagis cracked the front right fender on my Jeep. **[The end of John's first year in the Army!]**

December 26   Wednesday, We are all packed. There are about 40 trucks in a convoy. We came to Tsu. I led the convoy and drove [Capt.] Handell. The radios were in operation. There was snow in the mountains.

1945-10 John Carriker Jr [Nara, Japan, MP jeep of 369th FA, 98 Div]

1945-10 Osaka, Dad's jeep & a requisitioned Datsun auto

Yokohama in December 1945 [top]   and John & Sgt. Clyde J. Caskey [Kansas] in a park [below]

1945-late John Carriker Jr [inside burned out church, Yokohoma]

December 27   Thursday, I drove to Target 15 and got a saddle, some draftsman tools, rifles and swords.

> This was all that he wrote for this day! John participated in the disposal of Samurai swords, Cavalry swords, bayonets, Hari Kari knives and rifles. He was to lead a column of Jeeps and trucks full of them. They were in Nara and went to Tsu to get them. The Sergeant gave him papers and said "don't take any of them because they are numbered. Take them to Battalion Headquarters in Nara." John was leading the entire battery over a several day period. But he left Tsu by himself and headed home to Nara through the dirt mountain roads with the swords. He stopped on the side of the road and replaced one of his common swords with the best Samurai sword in the trailer so that the swords would still be numbered! After driving off, he rounded a bend in the road and came upon 3 officers in full uniform! They saw John's rifle [unloaded] and this fact and the noise of the Jeep scared the horses and officers off. He did not see them again. But they were not supposed to be in uniform 3 months after the end of the war. John went down the mountain. All in all, Dad had one Samurai sword and several other swords and knives. He got the rifles free. But all of the loads carried away by the American soldiers were burned in a pile and destroyed.

December 28   Friday, It was just a routine day. I closed in my Jeep.
December 29   Saturday, I thought of Don today and his birthday. I drove to Target 35 at the airfield.
December 30   Sunday, I drove back to the airfield to take [Capt.] Handell to Mass. I went to the Red Light District at night to check it. They are "off limits" and as the MP and Provost Marshall, I had to check them.
December 31   Monday, I didn't do much this morning. In the afternoon I took Sgt. Jordan to the Target 15-1-35 and 49, then ate supper.
January 1   Tuesday is NEW YEAR'S DAY, 1946. Today was supposed to be a holiday, but I drove just the same.
January 2   Wednesday, I took the sides off of the Jeep and cleaned it up. I hauled cinders today.
January 3   Thursday, 50 pointers left today. I'm back driving Major Zimmer now. Have a boy I have to clean for me. The Major sure is a nice fellow. I have filled up the photo albums. I drove to Matsusaka and got us a desk in the Corporal's room.
January 4   Friday, I got up and cleaned up the Major's room and left for Toba about 8:30 in the morning. I went to an ex-Marine training Camp (Target 9). I ate and was reminded of Toba Luru either in the hills or the bay. I went back up in the hills and Major bought a necklace. The town was on a bay about 25 miles from the highway. I drove back to Tsu, ate and sat around a charcoal pot and shot the breeze a while.
January 5   Saturday, I cleaned up the Major's room and sat around all morning. In the afternoon Major Zimmer and Capt Handell and an Interpreter and I went to a town called Ueno, up in the mountains through the tunnel and shopped for something. It sure was cold on the mountain. Ice 3' deep.
January 6   Sunday, I got up about 9:30 and loafed around and read all morning. I laid around all afternoon also.

1946 Mary Brachler at Red Cross Office in Yokohama

1946 Me and 1.5 ton truck in Yokohama

1946 Mary Brachler [widow] and Red Cross woman in Yokohama

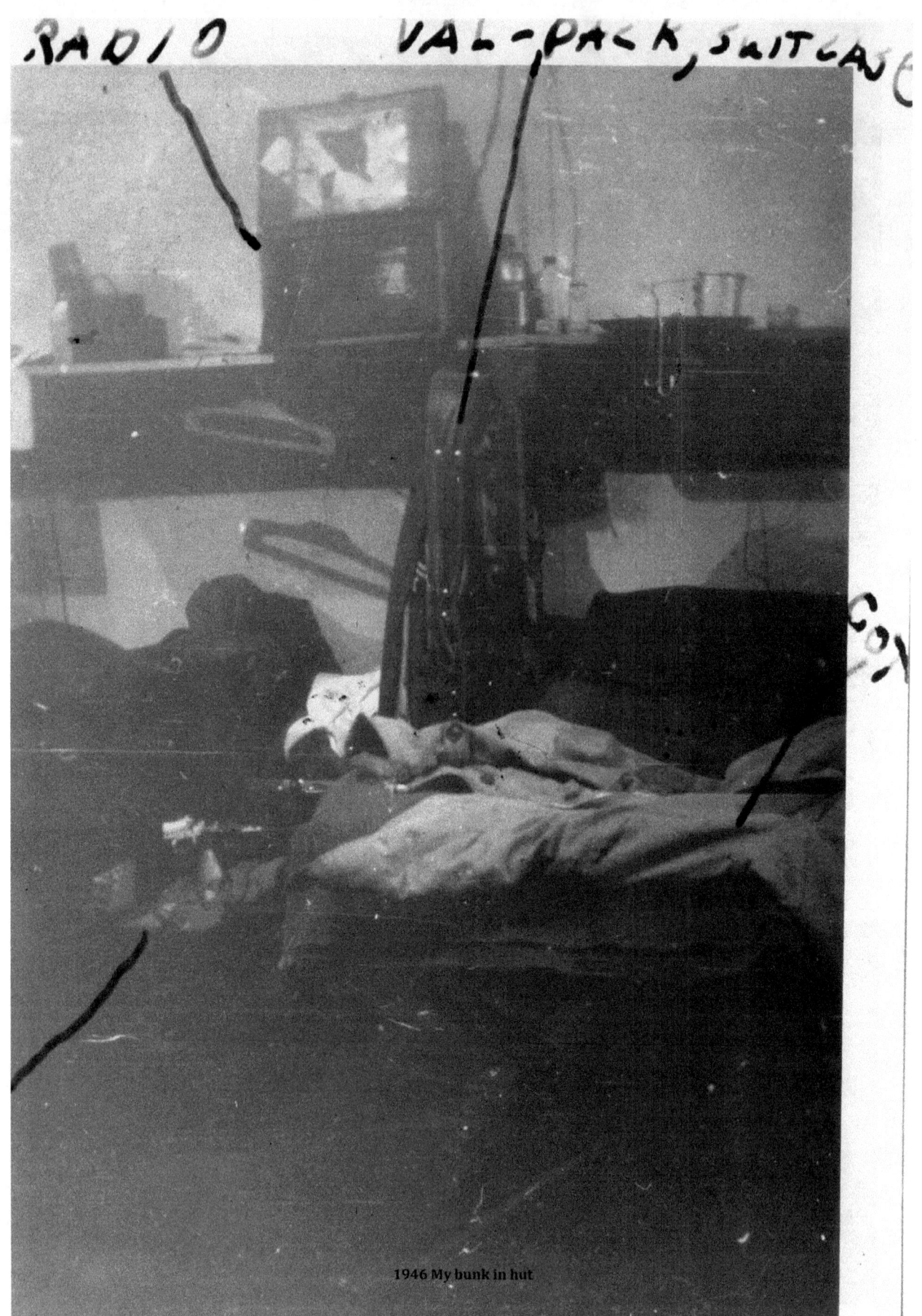

1946 My bunk in hut

January 7	Monday, I went to target 49 about a 45 minute ride north of here. I left my Jeep to close it in. I brought a C Battery Jeep [back to camp]. I saw the movie "**Summer Storm**" [Linda Darnell]. The girl looked like Candy. It certainly made me want to see Candy.

January 8	Tuesday, I went to the ammunition caves in the afternoon. That is about all.

January 9	Wednesday, It was a routine day. There was a plane crash.

January 10	Thursday, I did very little today and drove this morning to caves where ammunition is stored. I just laid around in the afternoon. Junior, the little Jap boy was on the switchboard and he said "New York?" Somebody was playing a joke on him. I saw the picture "**Scared Stiff**" and it was pretty good.

January 11	Friday, I just laid around all day long. We are all wondering what kind of congress is at home.

January 12	Saturday, In the morning I went to Target 49 after my Jeep. I got it about 10:30 and it sure is warm. The Mitsu-Bishi people built a Dur-aluminum body for it. I came back and ate and in the afternoon. Jack, Junior, the Interpreter and I went to Matsusake and got the silk parachute pajamas of Major's and I looked at some pearls for Major too. Bought 4 rolls of film.

January 13	Sunday, I slept till 10:30. I showered, sat around and ate dinner. After chow Crousby & I took some pictures here and also up by the anti-artillery guns that were destroyed. I ate chow and wrote letters. We discussed the Surcharge system Women's Home, etc.

January 14	Monday, I got up and lay around all morning. In the afternoon I took an interpreter to Matsusaki and we got the Flying Jackets. We drove back and let one interpreter go back with the Provost Marshall. I came on back to clean the stove and then ate chow and laid around.

January 15	Tuesday, Today I just cleaned up and fixed a tire. The Major wasn't here. I got 5 letters today: Mary Ann, Aunt Sue, Jim H., Dad and Ruth B. Mary Ann's letter sure was swell. I will certainly have to go see that little angel when I get home.

January 16	Wednesday, I drove Maj. Zimmer to Nagoya and to Osaka where 11 R.D. is. We got settled down to stay all night. I went to the Red Cross and ate my first ice cream since I got over here. I then went to bed.

January 17	Thursday, I got up and told Maj. Zimmer goodbye. I started back to Tsu and got to Tsu about noon. I packed up and started for Nara. I got lost up in the mountains and was running low on gas. I was ready to spend the night in the Jeep when I spotted [an American flag in the distance. It was Battalion Headquarters in] Nara. I finally made it with a quart of gas left.

January 18	Friday, I drove to Division Artillery and sat around all morning. (nothing in the afternoon) I almost died of homesickness at night and walked into town.

January 19	Saturday, I drove around with Sgt. Reese looking for lumber all morning. In the afternoon I took Maj. Simon to Osaka to take pictures. I got back and went on alert to go to town and Guard the jail to prevent some Chinese from being released.

January 20	Sunday, I went to church this morning. Chaplain Boutewell preached a good sermon. In the afternoon Caskey and I went to Nara on a pass and rode in a richshaw to took pictures. We walked around the park and saw <u>beautiful</u> Japanese girls from Yokohama.

January 21	Monday, I was on KP [Duty] all day and wrote a few letters.

January 22	Tuesday, I drove a messenger run all morning and afternoon. It was a nice though casual day. I read all night.

January 23	Wednesday, I drove Major. Simons to Division Artillery. I saw and ate with Arnold in Division Artillery.

1946 This was taken in Nara Park. I don't know the boy or girl. Caskey & I just snapped the photo because of the girl's good looks.

January 24   Thursday, I drove for Staff Sgt. Reese. I got the Plumbeys and Seamstresses; one was cute too. Sgt. Jordan told me to report in OD's [office] and I didn't. After supper, Ouch!

January 25   Friday, I bought water and drove for Maj. Simon to a train load of bulldozers. I drove to Division Artillery and took a girl home.

January 26   Saturday, I drove workers from Nara to camp and then drove Maj. Simon to a tailor shop, before and after dinner. Major Nesbitt, the Provost Marshall picked me up for driving on a street he claimed was off limits. Maj. Simon fixed it up though.

January 27   Sunday, I went to church this morning. It was a fine sermon. I wrote letters after dinner. I went to the hotel after the officers and talked with 2 Red Cross girls for quite a while.

January 28   Monday, I did very little today. I helped Caskey and took a seamstress back to town. I was on Fire Guard [Duty].

January 29   Tuesday, I took a convoy into town. It was a tractor 17-4 convoy with the 155mm [guns]. I drove to Division Artillery and was on Civil Patrol [Duty] all night.

January 30   Wednesday, I took the truck convoy to town. Vollmer drove a 2½ ton truck off the road and turned it over! I drove to Division Artillery, then ate and took a shower.

January 31   Thursday, I drove all around to Osaka this morning and Division Artillery in the afternoon.

February 1   Friday, I drove Tech. Sgt. Reese to Tsu in the morning. I was raining and snowing. We slid off the road once. I came back in the afternoon.

February 2   Saturday, I drove to Division Artillery in the morning and afternoon. At night I went to Jamicki and saw Hohenberger, Furguson, Spiner & Morris at Cobuct revue over at the NCO's and had a party.

February 3   Sunday, I went to church this morning and had communion. In the afternoon I drove to Nara and wrote letters.

February 4   Monday, I drove to Osaka in the morning and returned was cold. I was being transferred.

February 5   Tuesday, I went to Osaka with Stitt and Caskey to be transferred. Caskey got a swell deal in Division band. I was told I was to return to Nara and leave for Yokohama and be transferred to US ASCOM-C. I went to the Red Cross canteen and wrote letters, then ate, played records and returned to Nara.

February 6   Wednesday, everyone moved from Camp Mardin[1] to Camp Bennet 36-7. I am waiting on orders to come down to leave for Yokohama.

February 7   Thursday, I drove Capt. Daly this morning and heard him tell the new Major he wished he could give me to Major for his driver because I was one of the best drivers in the Division. I sure felt good that someone appreciated what efforts I do put forth.

February 8   Friday, I arrived at Yokohama about 8 o'clock and came to a Quonset hut and unpacked. I am assigned to the Red Cross as a Jeep driver for a cute brunette woman. What a racket! $100 a month pay! I saw the movie **"Under the Sun"** at the theatre. I had the 8th Army insignia sewn on.

---

[1] Camp Mardin established 10/14/1945 in memory of Clayton L. Mardin, First Lieutenant, Field Artillery USA, 98th Infantry Division, --Pilot of the 369th Field Artillery Battalion, killed in a plane crash on Oahu, Hawaii on 4 May 1945 while in training for action against the enemy."

1946 three girls that rode my jeep [Jeep-no]

1946-01 Sgt. Reese [Ohio] & my Jeep on top of Mtn at Uneo near Nara on way to Tsu.

February 9 — Saturday, I got up and ate and went to the Red Cross. I didn't do much, but got a shot this morning. In the afternoon I drove to Atsugi airfield and picked up a girl that just flew in. I saw 3 beautiful **USO** girls there. I went to the Red Cross after chow and had a bite to eat in our private little room.

February 10 — Sunday, I went to church and drove to the [Train] Station twice. I went to Tokyo after supper to take a girl home.

February 11 — Monday, I drove around all day, took workers home at night. Cute girl named Greto works there.

February 12 — Tuesday, I took 2 girls to Tokyo and one to Tochikama, then after supper took six girls to Tokyo with Bob. Cute one sat beside me. Ah-so.

February 13 — Wednesday, I drove to Tokyo after Mary Smith, 42nd and General Hospital. Drank my first 3 cokes in 6 months! Mary looked just like Betty Rae. Bob & I went to a show and saw **"Saratoga Trunk"** [with Gary Cooper & Ingrid Bergman]. Had the Jeep all night.

February 14 — Thursday, I drove the Jeep and fixed it up in the morning. I went to the station a few times and warehouse. Bob & I went to see **"San Antonio"** [Erroll Flynn & Alexis Smith] which was a good picture. Alexis Smith looks like Gloria.

February 15 — Friday, Today I drove Billie & Jane around about for a while and went to the warehouse. I went to a show at night **"Sailor takes a Wife"** with June Allyson and Bob Walker.

February 16 — Saturday, It is raining all day. I drove to Atsugi airfield after the Area Red Cross director ate there. I took him to Tokyo and got myself a coke on the way back. I went to the show again. I got a letter from Tinsy and from home.

February 17 — Sunday, I went to church this morning with Bob. When I woke up this morning, I saw four girls in the hut too. I just don't know what to think. I hung around the canteen all day and took some pictures. Went to see Betty Grable in **"The Diamond Horseshoe."** I took girls home.

February 18 — Monday, I took the Jeep to the motor pool. I took some girls home at night and saw a show **"Hold That Blonde"** with Eddie Bracken and Veronica Lake.

February 19 — Tuesday, I drove to Tokyo to PMO office and ate at the Imperial Hotel. I saw Mrs. [Jean Marie Faircloth] MacArthur and I saw Emperor Hirohito in his car. There was a long procession of cars. I went to the show (Bob & I) and saw Joan Leslie and Robert Alda and Alexis Smith in **"Rhapsody in Blue."** I sat behind a Capt and his girl and he couldn't get his arm around her because of my leg; more fun.

February 20 — Wednesday, I drove to 47th Replacement Depot and around town in the afternoon. I went to the show and saw **"Valley of Decision."** [Greer Garson & Gregory Peck]

February 21 — Thursday, I went after Billie and Jane and took them to the train. I sat around and in the afternoon drove around and got some mirrors for the Jeep. I went to the show with Bob to the Octagon Theatre. There was also a Jeep stage show and Betty Hutton was in **"Stork Club."**

February 22 — Friday, I drove around town and had a flat tire fixed. At night I took a Japanese Chorus girl to Tokyo after they gave a show at the Red Cross. **My drawing →**

February 23 — Saturday, I drove around town and in the afternoon I drove 3 girls to Tokyo and saw the cutest nurses. One of them spoke about me being in Corporal Breckenridge, KY because of my 98th Division patch.

Mrs. Jean MacArthur, son and Gen. MacArthur

IMPERIAL HOTEL, TOKYO, JAPAN　　　　　東京帝國ホテル

February 24	Sunday, I went to church this morning. I had the Jeep all afternoon and drove up on the cliff and looked at ships at sea. All week was just as uneventful a week. A couple of Tokyo trips and sat up to Ruth's house. Bob Stack, Wyatt and I had a nice talk on Sunday.

[February 25, 1946 – March 2, 1946   no dated entry]

March 3	Sunday, Snow is all over the ground. I drove to Kelly's house for a Japanese dinner with chop sticks. What a job! We had rice and meat, called Sukiyaki [すき焼き, a Japanese dish of cooked thinly sliced beef, rice, tofu, negi scallion, cabbage, noodles, soy sauce, sugar, mirin, placed on raw eggs]. Farmer, Ruth and I went to the Bankers Club and then back to Yokohama.

March 4	Monday, I had a 1½ ton truck and drove to Tokyo at night and took a girl to the train station.

March 5	Tuesday, I had Blakies ¾ ton truck and drove a girl to Tokyo and then to a show last night. I saw **"Gertie's Garters"** [Rosemary Theby].

March 6	Wednesday, I drove for Maggie Miller. I got bids for her without "feet" Ira! At the Brelux Theatre I went to see **"Week-end at the Waldorf."** [Ginger Rogers, Lana Turner, Walter Pigeon, Van Johnson]. It was a swell picture. It really made me homesick. I have another Jeep now. It is my 5th or 6th Jeep since last August. No mail at all anymore, hardly.

March 7	Thursday, I drove Billie & Jane to Tokyo early this morning. These two new girls are really nice; Sis & Mary, I think. Bob & I will try to take them out. I met an international French girl, a blonde, named Helen.

March 8	Friday, I took the winterizing off of the Jeep. I slept in bed sick as a horse.

March 9	Saturday, I drove a big run today up on the hill after the girls. I got winterizing for the Jeep today. I saw a show **"Janie gets Married."** I saw Sis & Mary after the show and at the house.

March 10	Sunday, I went to church this morning and just lay around today. I drove with Bob to take the girls home.

March 11	Monday, Today I drove around the 4th Rifle [Battalion-?] I had a flat tire on the Jeep, with no spare. I took the Canteen girls home and was told I was the driver of one of the new 1943 Mercury Station Wagons.

March 12	Tuesday, I drove the station wagon around and washed it. I drive to Tokyo each day. Tonight I went to the 4th Rifle. It sure was snowing. I saw Sis & had a talk with her.

March 13	Wednesday, Today I drove to Tokyo. I leave the Memorial Hall at 9:00am and arrive at the Theatre Headquarters building at 10 o'clock. I leave Tokyo at 1:30pm and get back to 2:30pm. I carry the Red Cross mail and passengers and took 5 today.

March 14	Thursday, I left for Tokyo at 9:00am as always and had 16 passengers. I came back empty.

March 15	Friday, I left empty this morning, only mail. I feel pretty low. The fever hit me in the after and at midnight, I got up, wrapped in a blanket and went outside and lost my supper. This is the first time that fever has hit hard since September.

March 16	Saturday, I left with four girls and 2 men this morning and came back with only mail. I am still quite sick. I saw the show **"Dolly Sisters"** [Betty Grable, John Payne, June Haver] with Bob.

March 17	Sunday, I went to church this morning and ate my first meal since Thursday noon. I am feeling a lot better.

1946-01 John Carriker Jr- Tokyo, Japan- Cpl Tech'n 5th grade

1946-01 Tokyo Zoo Park

Wooden Geta Shoe

1946-01, Cpl T5- 6 mo. John Carriker Jr -Yokahoma, Japan on European bluff [in front of burned out church]

March 18   Monday, I drove to Tokyo. It was rainy. There was not much business there. There sure is a beautiful girl in the Information Office. I saw Ginger Varutis & Deanna Durbin.

March 19   Tuesday, I drove to Tokyo. It is raining again. There is very little business. I drove girls to the station at night and saw Humphrey Bogart.

March 20   Wednesday, I drove to Tokyo and got mail. At last, five letters! It sure is swell to get mail again. I drove to the other side of Tokyo at night to a dance and got back around midnight.

March 21   Thursday, I drove to Tokyo with 2 men and 3 girls. We ate at the 5th Air Force. A live band and mess boys were there. I picked up a girl from Lesbon, Ohio and took her to her Billet. I then came back and drove to Atsugi Airfield and then took a shower.

March 22   Friday, I left for Tokyo and took 3 girls and 1 man to town. I took Miss Todd to the 42nd General Hospital [built by Proctor & Gamble]. I washed the Mercury and had the tires rotated.

March 23   Saturday, I was up about 2:00 for Guard [Duty]. I sneaked about 2½ hours of sleep in though. I left for Tokyo with 1 girl and 2 men and picked up 5 Hawaiian girls in Tokyo. I came back to find Sis & Mary had been in an accident. They seem to be ok now though. It rained all day. I got a 9-day letter. It sure is good to hear from home again.

March 24   Sunday, A farmer got me up and asked if I would like to take my Mercury to Tokyo and take Sis & Mary to the Hospital. Of course I jumped out of bed. I got Sis & Mary in the car and the poor kids were really hurting, especially Mary. She has a dislocated shoulder. I took them to Tokyo to the hospital, about a 22 mile ride over a rough road. Each bump I hit, I could see Mary, sitting beside me, winch with pain. It took about an hour and a half to get there. I drove very slow so as not to bounce them around too much. In front of the 42nd General Hospital I helped Mary out and she almost fainted. We started down the hall and Mary did faint on me and I eased her to the floor and they brought a stretcher for her. We got her in bed and Sis and the Navy man and I ate and drove back to Yokohama. I took Sis home from chow and when she went to get out of the 1½ ton truck I had, her legs were up that she couldn't bend them, so I put my arms around her and lifted her down. That was the first time in 10 months I had even come close to having my arms around a girl. Sis & Mary are really swell girls. They have been swell to me.

March 25   Monday, I left for Tokyo empty except for mail and my fever which has hit me again. I'm taking sulfur pills again. They sure do leave you weak. I delivered the mail and took 4 or 5 letters to Mary in the Hospital. She sure looked a lot better. She seemed glad to see me. I don't see why they think I'm doing so much for them. Mary said she would like Sis to send her some stationary, so I went to the PX and bought her some and some candy and magazines. I know how lonely these hospitals are. Besides, I like Mary and Sis pretty well, probably better than is good for me. I'm just 21 and they are 24 & 25 and besides I'm no officer, just and old T5 enlisted man.

March 26   Tuesday, I took three people in today. I'm sure feeling rough. I went to see Mary. She was looking a lot better and it sure is strange, but she seems so glad to see me.

March 27   Wednesday, I took seven people to Tokyo and saw a man get hit by a truck, a huge fire and then I went to see Mary at the hospital. I sure do like her. She was sitting up this morning and seemed better. We had a nice long talk. I took her two letters and she again talked of how glad she was to see me. I came back to Yokohama, left for Atsugi Airfield and took a lady out there. I came back and had 9 letters!

1946-01-26 following a Honey Wagon on Enoshima Island, Japan

1946-02 My hut in Yokahama, Japan

1946-01 This is the room we had at Tsu in Japan

1946-03 John A. Carriker, Jr. is driving in Tokyo in an early 1940's Mercury wagon that carries 8 passengers.

1946-03 The Imperial Hotel where I eat when in Tokyo

March 28   Thursday, I took 2 men today and went to the PX and got my pictures (not bad) then took some magazines and candy to Mary up in the hospital. She sure is swell. I got there about a quarter of ten and left at 1:10pm in the afternoon. The nurse said she would watch for the Doc in case he came & she closed the door (these weren't visiting hours). I sure do like Mary. I got back [to Yokohama] and went to Atsugi Airfield and back and saw a show **"The Call of the Wild"** [Clark Gable, Loretta Young, Jack Oakie].   I got 5 rolls of film, a real package and 11 letters.

March 29   Friday, Today, I went to Tokyo and saw Mary. She was unhappy I could see, but I tried my best to cheer her up. I sure do like her. I brought her back to Yokohama, of course, she sat beside me and kidded me all the way. I sure do like her.

March 30   Saturday, I drove to Tokyo with Bob and Takeo. We delivered mail and I saw Jim Nelson in the hospital. It was the first time I've seen him in a year. I drove back and had a flat tire with no spare. I got the Japs to fix it and got back and Mary had left me a note thanking me and giving me a carton of Camels and a beautiful Hanson lighter. I love her. She is such a wonderful friend she is. I didn't see her all day. I don't know when I'll see her next. I got 32 letters today. I sure do like them.

March 31   Sunday, I went to church with Mary this morning. She sure is wonderful. I felt so good setting beside her. I took her home we had a wonderful talk. She was telling me all about her husband. She is so sweet. Bob and I went to take pictures this afternoon, then took a nap. I saw Anita again. Anita is Mary & Sis's friend.

April 1   Monday, I drove to Tokyo with Bob. We drove around and picked up "Totsi" now! We came back and picked up 2 girls and Sis at the train station. Sis & Mary are so swell.

April 2   Tuesday, I went to Tokyo again and drove "Totsi" around & she was really ok. I saw **"TARS & SPARS"** today [Janet Blair, Alfred Drake & Marc Platt].

April 3   Wednesday, I drove to Tokyo and took "Totsi" out again and her boy. I met her sister… really cute too! I saw the **USO** show "Red, Hot & Blue," a colored variety show with Doris Wood as a Zoot suiter [Betty Hutton, Victor Mature, William Demarest, June Havoc]. It sure was a swell show.

April 4   Thursday, I went to Tokyo again and took "Totsi" to Oh Yes, out for a drive with her. She is really cute. I went to a party at Ruth's house tonight. It was pretty nice.

April 5   Friday, I drove to Tokyo again. The weather is wonderful. I ate and came back after supper. I went up after Mary at the train station. I got on the cars to help her with her bags and she ran to me and thrust her arms around me and of course then I did the same. Only Sis and that Lieutenant took her with them. The Lieutenant is another of the so called lonely married boys---baloney!!! I've driven officers too long and heard them give out with that same line too many times to believe it. Bob & I saw **"Abilene Town"** [Randolph Scott, Lloyd Bridges, Ann Dvorak]. It was a pretty good movie.

April 6   Saturday, I drove in [to Tokyo] with one girl this morning and saw the 1st Cavalry Division parade by MacArthur's Building. I took some pictures and went to eat and saw [Gen.] Montgomery and Leonard Hohenburger. I drove all around and came back empty. Bob & I went to see **"Ziegfeld Follies"** [William Powell, Judy Garland, Lucille Ball]. I got my pictures today- Mary's are swell!

April 7   Sunday, I went to church this morning and came back and ate and then I wrote letters to Skippy, Mary Ann & Aunt Sue.

April 8   Monday, I went to Tokyo and bought a blue kimono for myself at the PX. Nothing new today.

April 9   Tuesday, I took Jeanne & 4 girls and 1 man over to Tokyo today and saw "Totsi." Oh baby!

1946-03 The Imperial Hotel where I eat when in Tokyo

1946-03 This is the Red Cross Building I drive to every morning.
It is the Pacific Theatre Hdqs of Red Cross for Japan and Korea

1946-04 Army Day Parade in Tokyo

1946-04 Church [St. Andrews EC] ruins in Yokohama

1946-04 Church ruins [St. Andrews EC] in Yokahama, Japan

1946-04 Dad at Buddha at Komakura [nr. Yokohoma]

April 10   Wednesday, I broke the radiator so I had to take a ¾ ton truck to Tokyo today. I got some silk pajamas and arranged to see Chaplain Cartwright tomorrow. Bob & I saw **"Up Goes Maisie"** [Ann Sothern, George Murphy, Hillary Brooke] at the Octagon Theatre.

April 11   Thursday, I took 3 girls to Tokyo and went to see Chaplain Cartwright. I sure had a very nice talk. I went to the PX and back after "Totsi" and went for a ride. Anita & Sis & Mary want Bob & I to go to the show with them tomorrow night. OH baby! I don't know why but I went to the Cemetery of the Army and found Lt. Houghton, joining brothers, grave later. I found out it was a year ago tonight he died.

April 12   Friday, I drove to Tokyo with 2 girls and got a haircut for my date tonight. Bob & I went after Sis & Mary. They were really beautiful. Mary had a rose in her hair, combed long and a bright red coat. She looked very beautiful. We saw the show **"They were Expendable"** [John Wayne, Robert Montgomery, Donna Reed].Went up to their house afterwards and ate sandwiches and sat in a small living room and talked, then came home.

April 13   Saturday, I drove in this morning and came back and took pictures up to Mary. She & I & Bob looked them over and then Anita & Mary & Bob and I went to the cemetery and took pictures of it and John Houghton's grave. Bob & I saw a **USO** show **"Panama Hattie"** [Red Skelton, Ann Sothern] and the picture **"Scarlet Street"** [Edward G. Robinson, Joan Bennett].

April 14   Sunday, Bob & I went to church this morning on "Palm Sunday". It was a good sermon. We saw Sis & Mary after church for a second. Bob & I ran around and took pictures in the afternoon. I went to sleep early.

April 15   Monday, I took 7 girls to Tokyo. Larry sure got Cora Smith, a cute **USO** girl. We rode around with her quite a bit and also Kay Medford, the actress. Bob & I went to the train station and took some girls. I haven't seen Sis or Mary Today.

April 16   Tuesday, was just an ordinary day. There was nothing much doing. I saw "Panama Hattie" again, with some cute girl in it [Ann Sothern].

April 17   Wednesday, It is pouring down rain! I took Mr. Phillips to Tokyo today and saw Mary and she says she is being transferred to Sendai. I sure hate to see her go. I like her an awful lot.

April 18   Thursday, I drove to Tokyo as usual and came back. I went to see Mary and took Sis & Mary to the Commissary. It sure was nice. Tomorrow night we take them to the train station.

April 19   Friday, I drove in to Tokyo as usual and came back.. I took Mary and the girl to Tokyo to catch the train for Sendai. I sure hated to say goodbye to them. The train pulled out and I felt terrible. She was so nice to me. It was a lonely trip back to Yokohama with the moon out.

April 20   Saturday, I drove my car in to Tokyo as usual with nothing exciting. Bob & I saw **"ABC's of the USA"** and **"Life with Blondie."**

April 21   Sunday, I went to church and took a nap in the afternoon. I wrote a few letters.

April 22   Monday, [I went to] Tokyo as usual, with nothing at all exciting. Bob & I saw a Japanese movie tonight. It was really a scream about a little wrestler.

April 23   Tuesday, I went to Tokyo and took Miss Todd and Mr. Walker. Bob & I went to see Jeanne Crain, Dana Andres & Dick Haymes in **"State Fair."** It was really swell.

April 24   Wednesday, I drove in [to Tokyo] as usual. It sure was windy. I saw a **USO** show, **"Gilbert & Leo's Variety."**

April 25   Thursday, It is pouring down rain. There was nothing unusual except the car quit on me; it was the distributor.

April 26   Friday, I drove in [to Tokyo] as usual and took one of the other cars. Nothing at all happened today. Bob & I saw **"The Bells of St. Mary"** [Bing Crosby, Ingrid Bergman, Henry Travers].

OCTAGON THEATRE AT ISEZAKI STREET

The Octagon Theater was named when the 8th Army came to Japan [notice its symbol].
The theater had another name before and after the occupation.

John Houghton was the navigator on a B-29 on a bombing mission to the Tokyo area. Prior to the end of the war his plane was shot down and his remains interred in the American Cemetery in Yokohama. Dad was good friends with Jim Houghton, John's younger brother, in Marion, Ohio, where Jim and Dad graduated together from High School. Dad and Red Cross Nurse, Mary, went to the cemetery to find his grave, which had just been made the day before. Before this Mrs. Houghton, who was a widow, had only been told that her son was shot down. Now she would hear that he gave his life for sake of our freedom and the freedom of the Japanese people.

1946-04 Jailbirds with Japanese straw sacks over their heads. They are supposed to be ashamed of themselves.

1946-04 Myself in Yokohama

April 27 — Saturday, the car fan quit on me, so I didn't run around much. I drove back slow and saw a show **"Junior Miss"** [Peggy Ann Garner, Stephen Dunne, Allyn Joslyn]. It was really swell.

April 28 — Sunday, I went to church this morning and loafed the rest day and saw **"Behind Green Light"** [Carole Landis, William Gargan, Richard Crane].

April 29 — Monday, I drove to Tokyo today and picked up Pat Smith, a **USO** girl that played in **"Panama Hattie"** (**USO** show #772). She is really cute. I also met the man that played the sailor, Charlie is his name.

April 30 — Tuesday, I drove to Tokyo as usual and went out to see Charlie. I ate dinner with him and drove uptown and mailed a package.

May 1 — Wednesday, I drove in [to Tokyo] as usual and saw Charlie again & we went and bought my Tropical Worsted Sun Tans [suits, $27.50]. They are really nice. Charlie leaves tomorrow for Kyoto.

May 2 — Thursday, I drove in as usual and drove around. I saw the May Day Parades. There were half a million Japanese parading around. 2 GI's were beat up by 100 Japanese. I saw a show **"Colonel Effingham's Raid"** [Charles Coburn, Joan Bennett, William Eythe].

May 3 — Friday, I drove in with 7 passengers today, fooled around and had a flat tire on my way tire on my way back. I saw a show **"Whistle Stop"** [Ava Gardner, George Raft, Victor McLaglen].

May 4 — Saturday, I drove in [to Tokyo] as usual today. There was nothing unusual that happened.

May 5 — Sunday, I went to church this morning in the little chapel by the office. I drove to Ryugasaki this afternoon. It is on the other side of Tokyo.

May 6 — Monday, I drove in as Usual and in the afternoon I went back to Tokyo. After the **USO** show **"Harlem Varieties,"** Ida Jones, etc., I took them back.

May 7 — Tuesday, A farmer smashed my car this morning. I drove in [to Tokyo] as usual. Bob is dating Peggy and I saw **"Arsenic and Old Lace"** [Cary Grant, Priscilla Lane, Raymond Massey].

May 8 — Wednesday, I drove in as usual to Tokyo.

May 9 — Thursday, I drove in as usual and took the mail, etc., and delivered it. Hemorrhoids have been bad all week. I went to the doctor and got some salve.

May 10 — Friday, I drove in [to Tokyo] today in a lot of rain and after supper, Bob, Peggy and I rode around and got a coke and saw a little puppy.

May 11 — Saturday, I drove to Tokyo as usual and took a girl and 2 men. I saw General Eisenhower close enough to touch him, at General McArthur's office. I came back and Bob and I went to see a **USO** show **"Drum Boogie."**

May 12 — Sunday, I got up and went to church for a fine Mother's Day sermon. I ate dinner and wrote letters.

May 13 — Monday, I drove in to Tokyo as usual. It is raining a lot these days.

May 14 — Tuesday, I drove in to Tokyo as usual. It is raining a lot these days.

May 15 — Wednesday, I drove in to Tokyo as usual. It is raining a lot these days.

May 16 — Thursday, I drove in as usual and fooled around a lot. At night I went to a show called **"Co-eds."** It was real good. Sweaters & skirts--- ah! Also saw **"Adventure"** with Clark Gable and Greer Garson [& Joan Blondell].

May 17 — Friday, It is raining as usual. I drove around town and went to the **USO** show **"Cybil Broerns Co-Eds."** It was really good: girls in sweaters and skirts.

1946-04 Ruins of 2 story house in Yokohama

1946-04 Yokohama with hill in background

1x11, 2x11, April 4, 1946. Punaluu. Houses and highway were about 5-6 feet above sea level here. No well defined debris lines remain but the wave was apparently about 12 feet in height. Houses were destroyed, automobiles overturned, and trees uprooted. The wave struck here with considerable force and flooded back into the cane fields a distance of about 1500 feet from the sea.

3x11, 4x11, April 4, 1946. Punaluu.

1946-04-17 Bombed out church [St. Andrews EC] in Yokohama

1946-05 British [Indian] soldiers in parade in Tokyo

The 2nd Battalion, 5th Royal Gurkha Rifles marching through Kure soon after their arrival in Japan. (May 1946)

1946-05 US Army Cemetery, Yokahama, Japan

May 18	Saturday, I drove in with 7 girls off of the ship that wanted to go singing. We drove around town and sat. I went to bed early.
May 19	Sunday, I went to church this morning. It was a good sermon on **"The Mind of Repentance."** I ate dinner and went to the swimming pool. It is a beautiful pool surrounded on 3 sides by ills. It sure was swell.
May 20	Monday, I drove to Tokyo as usual and met Lou Litwin, a **USO** man in "Ginhom Girl."
May 21	Tuesday, I too Lou & Johnny Ostrium (from Miami and the band leader) up town. He gave me 3 shirts and 1 pair of pants. At the show I stood in line from 5 till 7 to get in and 7 till 8 for the show. I had a front row seat and saw 2 ex-Rockettes in the **"Ginhom Girl"** show. One brunette is Dorothy Dill.
May 22	Wednesday, [I went to] Tokyo as usual and took Lou uptown. I ate dinner at the Table with "Tootsie, a riot." Tonight, Bob and I came back for a walk to the truck and I found a Jap stealing a can of pipe tobacco, so we made him shine all our shoes then made him eat the box of tobacco. He was really sick; sweat was all over him. He was an ex-soldier and had a rank chart on him. I'll bet he never ever thinks of chewing tobacco again.
May 23	Thursday, I drove to Tokyo as usual and Lou and I found a lake where we rowed around in a boat. I saw **"Masquerade in Mexico"** [Dorothy Lamour, Arturo De Cordova, Patric Knowles].
May 24	Friday, I drove in [to Tokyo] as usual and rode around in a new Mercury. Bob and I saw **"Sentimental Journey"** [John Payne, Maureen O'Hara, William Bendix].
May 25	Saturday, I drove in with Bob today. He, Lou and a **USO** girl and I went to the District Building, equivalent to the Capital [Building] and went through its Art Museum.
May 26	Sunday, I went to church and in the afternoon, Bob and I varnished the Mercury. It sure looks swell at night. We went on a freight ship and went through it: engine room, control room, radio room and map room.
May 27	Monday, [I went to] Tokyo as usual. There was nothing much doing.
May 28	Tuesday, [I went to] Tokyo again and saw Lou again and went uptown. I danced at night at the Yokohama Club.
May 29	Wednesday, [I went to] Tokyo again and saw Lou. I didn't do much.
May 30	Thursday, There was no work today. Bob, Jimmy, Lowry, Avery and I went to Tokyo and rowed around in the river there in a boat apiece, it was near a dam. I went to the pool in the afternoon and saw a show **"Murder in the Music Hall"** at night [Vera Ralston, William Marshall, Helen Walker].
May 31	Friday, I drove in as usual and drove around. At night Bob and I went to the show with bicycle riders doing 27 different swings with no hands. We also saw the movie **"Tangier"** [Maria Montez, Robert Page, Sabu].
June 1	Saturday, I drove in as usual and had 3 Australian actresses dressed as nurses. I moved to the new [Quonset] hut area. The beds have springs! It is the first time in over a year almost.
June 2	Sunday, I went to church this morning and back to chow. Went rowing in the afternoon on the river near Tokyo and found a miniature Coney Island, improvised roller coaster and whip Ferris wheel, airplanes, merry-go-round; a very unique and primitive sight. I saw **"The Spiral Staircase"** with Dorothy McGuire [George Brent, Ethel Barrymore].

1946-06 Bombed out area with burned out church remaining intact- Yokohama

1946-06 Japanese woman carrying baby- all babies are carried like this- Tokyo

1946-06-15 Tokyo Zoo

June 3   Monday, I drove to Tokyo alone with the mail this morning and read books on Physical Science and the part on the Solar System. I brought George back and we all went to Ordinance for 12 Jeeps. We brought them all back to the Officer's [Quarters]. I got paid and sent $290.80 home by money order.

June 4   Tuesday, I drove in to Tokyo as usual. Nothing important happened.

June 5   Wednesday, I drove in to Tokyo as usual. Nothing important happened.

June 6   Thursday, I drove in to Tokyo as usual. Nothing important happened.

June 7   Friday, I drove in to Tokyo as usual. Nothing important happened. I saw **"Spellbound"** at night [Ingrid Bergman, Gregory Peck, Michael Chekov].

June 8   Saturday, I drove in to Tokyo as usual. Nothing important happened.

June 9   Sunday, I went to church this morning at Memorial Hall. I ate chow and loafed around in the afternoon. I saw an International Male chorus and Gene Tierney in **"Dragonwyck"** [Walter Huston, Vincent Price, Glenn Langan].

June 10   Monday, I drove in as usual to Tokyo and putted around. I came back and Farmer and I went swimming. Then we, Breson, Stuck, Farmer & I, went to Tokyo after **USO** girls in 2½ ton, 1½ ton and ¾ ton trucks. I drove the 2½ ton truck back. Boy did we have fun.

June 11   Tuesday, I drove into Tokyo with 1 girl and took mail as always. I ate ice cream in the PX and came back and went to the show **"Ideal Girl."** It was pretty good. I got a letter from Gloria inviting me to a birthday party.

June 12   Wednesday, I drove in as usual and saw Pat Smith, a small **USO** girl. I ate ice cream and picked up Farmer & Larry and we all ate and went out to the **USO** Station and then to the Zoo. We came back and had a flat tire. The show was **"Hoodlum Saint"** with William Powell and Esther Williams [Angela Lansbury]. I woke up at 12:30am as sick as I could be. I was feeling terrible!

June 13   Thursday, I drove in as usual. I am still sick from last night. I looked around and came back and saw a boxing match at the open air theatre.

June 14   Friday, I drove in as usual and after supper Bob & I drove to Tokyo. I went to the PX and saw a girl that looks like Dorothy Smith. She sure is cute.

June 15   Saturday, I drove in with 6 girls and Bob. We drove around Tokyo and ate ice cream at the PX and dinner at the Air Force Mess Hall. We came back and saw Yvonne De Carlo in **"Frontier Gal"** [Rod Cameron, Andy Devine]. It sure was a swell picture.

June 16   Sunday, I went to church and heard 21 mostly men go hazmu and had Ruth's Jeep for the afternoon, night and morning. Bob & I went to Tokyo and saw the Museum and Uno Zoo. We drove around and went to see the Ernie Pyle [memorial] and then back to Yokohama. We drove around for a while and Bob tried to lose me in his 1½ ton truck, but couldn't do it.

June 17   Monday, I drove to Tokyo and had a flat tire in Tokyo and on the way back I had a blowout outside of Yokohama. I was only driving around 35 mph so I got stopped OK. We got a sleeping sickness shot. It was the worst I've ever had. It burned for a long time.

June 18   Tuesday, I went to Tokyo as usual. I wasn't feeling so good. Bob & I went to see **"Maldowes Secret"** at the Memorial Hall.

June 19   Wednesday, I went to Tokyo again and drove around. I had a flat tire and a blowout on the Mercury. Bob & I went to see **"Cornered"** at the Octagon [Dick Powell, Walter Selzak, Micheline Cheirel].

June 20   Thursday, I went to Tokyo as usual. I saw Emperor Hirohito today and the Japanese diet at their equivalent to our Capital. I walked to take my laundry and sat on deck watching harbor ships.

Ernie Pyle Memorial

1946-06-21 One Entrance to the Emporer's Palace

1946-08 Part of Parade in Yokohama- Indian soldiers

1946-6-22 Enoshima Beach on Enoshima Island

1946-06-21 Meiji Building- Pacific Air Command Headquarters, Tokyo

1946-06-23 Entrance to Temple on Enoshima Island

June 21   Friday, I went to Tokyo as usual. It is very hot out. I came back and Avery & I rode around after supper. Another girl was in the hut tonight.
June 22   Saturday, I drove in to Tokyo and saw a Jeep and a ¾ ton truck burn up at Hobyo Hall. I came back and drove to Tokyo at night. She is a swell girl in the PX snack bar there.
June 23   Sunday, I drove to church then after dinner I drove to Kamakure and ran up and down the beach in our Jeep. I climbed the Mountain of Enoshima there also.
June 24   Monday, I drove to Tokyo with 1 girl and saw a Jap get hit in Tokyo. A GI ambulance got him. I ate and drove back, but the radiator was bad. I filled 4 times today. [Military] Wives arrived this morning about 8:30am. I got a shave.
June 25   Tuesday, I drove to Tokyo as usual. I got a ticket for running a red light and saw a parade and defendants [of the War Crimes Trial]. Bob & I took Ruth to the Country Club and Bob went back after her. We saw a dead Japanese man being pulled out of the canal.
June 26   Wednesday, I saw them pull a Japanese girl out of the canal this morning. She was very stiff and almost black. I drove to Tokyo with Jane Bradley. We had coffee at the Banks Club and had a nice talk. I came back and saw a show **"Swing Parade of 1946"** [Gale Storm, Phil Regan, Moe Howard].
June 27   Thursday, I drove to Tokyo again and had ice cream at the PX. I drove around, ate dinner and came back. I went to see Larry at the hospital and them to the show **"Bad Bascomb"** with Wallace Berry and Margaret O'Brien [Marjorie Main].
June 28   Friday, I drove to Tokyo again and had Miss Todd again to take to 42nd General Hospital. I saw a British Parade at the Imperial Palace Grounds. There were a lot of wives of the men there. I came back to Yokohama and saw the play **"Drunkard"** and the show **"Little Giant"** with Abbott & Costello [Brenda Joyce].
June 29   Saturday, I drove to Tokyo again and ran around, ate and came back. I got the Jeep and Bob & I went to Tokyo again. We came out of a snack bar and found a body in the back of the Jeep. It scared us to death! I got an MP and it turned out to be an awfully feeble old man. They took him to the Provost Marshall Office. We saw a short film on Ernie Pyle and then went home.
June 30   Sunday, I went to church, then worked on seat covers on the Jeep. Bob & I went to the new Enlisted Men's Club in Yokohama. It sure is a nice club there. We rode up on the Mountains to some huge double-barrel coastal guns. Then we came home.
July 1   Monday, I went to Tokyo with 1 lady and came back to Yokohama. I got a ticket for not wearing a hat while driving! I am feeling quite sick. The radio just made an announcement that men with 20 months by September 30 will be on their way [home] by the 20th of September! [Actually, the 13th of September!] That is wonderful news!! Bob Trehka, Bob Hottie and I drove to Yokohama and back and saw Alan Ladd and Veronica Lake [William Bendix] in **"Blue Dahlia."** It was good! We came back to the hut about 11 o'clock. I heaved and was quite sick.   [74 days until departure!]
July 2   Tuesday, I am feeling quite sick today. I have been for two weeks now. I went to Tokyo to see a Doctor and came back. He said I am nervous. He gave me some medicine. I saw a movie **"Her Kind of Man"** [Dane Clark, Janis Page, Zachary Scott].
July 3   Wednesday, I went to Tokyo again and it is raining. I took Dan, the paratrooper, along. I got some medicine from the Doctor for my stomach and nerves. I have a splitting headache and went to bed early.
July 4   Thursday, I slept until 9 o'clock. I am feeling quite rough today. I drove around to a show in the afternoon [no name] and night too [no name].

1946-06-23 Enoshima Island, Japan

1946-06-23 Enoshima Island Beach, Japan

1946-06-23 View from the top of the mountain on Enoshima Island, Japan

1946-08 Buddha idol in Kamakura

1946-08 Japanese boys carrying an idol like the girls do

1946-08 Small girls carrying an idol- a few would pull down on it & others pretended to make great sacrifice while chanting, Tokyo

July 5 	Friday, I went to Tokyo as usual and it is raining again. I am feeling a little better and saw a show at the Octagon [no name]. 	[10 weeks until departure]

July 6 	Saturday, I went to Tokyo with Bob today. I got Ruth and the Jeep and went to out NCO Club and show.

July 7 	Sunday, I went to church and after dinner went swimming. Jimmie & Stuck dunked Bob over 100 times. We saw the show **"Fear"** [Peter Cookson, Warren William, Anne Gwynne]. [75 days until departure!]

July 8 	Monday, I drove to Tokyo as usual. It is pouring down rain! I was called into Major Hopes office about the ticket. I am having my Val-Pack printed. I saw a show- short, at the Recreation Hall.

July 9 	Tuesday, I drove to Tokyo as usual. It was drizzling. Miss Todd, Ruth & Mrs. Nadeau went with me. There was a BTO's meeting at the Bankers' Club. I came back and saw a show **"Gay Blades"** [Allan Lane, Jean Rogers, Edward Ashley]. I am still feeling rough.

July 10 	Wednesday, I drove to Tokyo again. Accustomed to pretty hot, but I felt quite sick and offered a prayer and have felt much better since. My ticket for driving with a hat came to Ruth so I got out of it. I sat around out front of the hut till 9:00pm and went to bed.

July 11 	Thursday, Reveille at 6:00am always. I ate breakfast and am feeling much better. I believe faith has a lot to do with it. I went to Tokyo again. There was nothing unusual. I saw **"Gay Blades"** again. Blair was out today.

July 12 	Friday, I went to Tokyo in "51C738" and had a flat tire. The fan belt pully broke, the ignition system broke, so I had it towed by a wrecker from the Bankers Club back to Yokohama. I saw **"My Sister Eileen"** [Rosalind Russell, Brian Aherne, Janet Blair] and **"The Well Groomed Bride"** [Olivia de Havilland, Ray Milland, Sonny Tufts]. 	[9 weeks to departure!]

July 13 	Saturday, I went to Tokyo this morning. The radiator hose came off the block 3 times! I finally fixed it. I ate lunch and saw "Totsi". I came back and Bob & I ate. Then I cleaned up and went to bed.

July 14 	Sunday, I went to church in the morning and wrote Mom & Dad. I then ate chow and laid around the hut all afternoon and night.

July 15 	Monday, I went to Tokyo again and saw Marie at the Bankers Club. There are more beautiful Japanese girls at the Bankers Club! The oil seal on the front right wheel is leaking so I put the car in the garage. I guess I'll use the Jeep tomorrow. Ruth and Farmer came back today. I saw a show **"Dark Corner"** with Lucille Ball and William Bendix [Clifton Webb, Mark Stevens].

July 16 	Tuesday, I went to Tokyo again. There was nothing unusual. I had a few nice looking girls in the Jeep today. I came back and got another shot today: "Ee-ty." Then Bob & I rode around after the show and then I went to bed. There was nothing exciting that happened all day.

July 17 	Wednesday, I went to Tokyo again. Bilew, Sallicorn & I had coffee at the back room of the Bankers Club. Nothing unusual happened today. Bob & I saw Judy Garland in **"Harvey Girls"** [Ray Bolger, John Hodiak].

July 18 	Thursday, Seeing as I am the Squad Leader, I have to sound Reveille! I took the grey ambulance to Tokyo today. Riccardi rode in my car. It was very hot out. The heat, I think, is the most I've ever endured outside of Texas!

1946-08 Japanese Priest in a celebration, some sort of 3 day festival, Tokyo

1946-08 Japanese Priests, Tokyo

1946-08 My bunk and locker in Yokohama

1946-08 Temple Grounds at Komakura

1946-08 Tokyo street scene

1946-08 Victory Banquet held by Japanese in Manila- painting by Japanese painter in Tokyo's Uneo Museum [Tojo, Yamashita]

July 19   Friday, I got up and ate breakfast and went to Tokyo as usual. I ate lunch and came back and drove Mrs. Kirkland, Miss Foster & 5 other women to the Ernie Pyle Memorial in Tokyo to the **"Eye of the Future"** contest. I saw a show **"Tarzan and the Leopard Women"** [Johnny Weissmuller, Brenda Joyce, Johnny Sheffield]. I got back and drank Cokes with no ice cubes. I was up 11-3 billet and got in about 12:00am.   [8 weeks to departure!]

July 20   Saturday, I was up as usual at 6:00am for Reveille. I drove to Tokyo with Ginny Sledge of Charlotte, NC, so we had a nice talk about North Carolina [The Carrikers were from NC and John, Jr. had visited there, but never lived there]. I took 2 girls to the pool. I went to the pool in Tokyo and then went back to Yokohama.. I ate supper with Bob and we got in the Jeep and saw a girl at the point where we watch ships at the South Pier. I saw a show with Lana Turner in **"The Postman Always Rings Twice"** [John Garfield, Cecil Kellaway].

July 21   Sunday, I went to church this morning and ate dinner in the afternoon with Bob. I drove Ruth's Jeep to Kamakura, a summer resort on the ocean, and Bob & I went in swimming in the afternoon. I saw **"The Bride Wore Boots"** [Barbara Stanwyck, Robert Cummings, Diana Lynn]. It sure was good.

July 22   Monday, I sounded Reveille and they made us march on the street too. I went to Tokyo as usual and went to the Bankers Club and went across the street and ate. I came back and Bob & I rode bicycles in uptown Yokohama.

July 23   Tuesday, I went to Tokyo as usual and rode around and took 3 girls back to Yokohama. Bob & I drove around at night.

July 24   Wednesday, I went to Tokyo again. It is still as hot as it can be! The humidity is terrible- 81^0-96^0 so far during the days. It is the hottest I've ever seen. Helen Ambrose and I picked up this priest and went to find the Sacred Heart Convent. Then I ate and came back. Bob & I did nothing but ride around.

July 25   Thursday, I went to Tokyo as usual and went to see War Crimes Trials. [General] Tojo and all the war prisoners were there. The Judges and Defense Counsels were fighting back and forth. The Judge was British. The Counselor was an American. I came back and rode around, then went to bed.

July 26   Friday, I went to Tokyo again. Miss Todd & Helen Ambrose went along. I came back and played Solitaire. Bob & I went to see June Allyson in **"Two Sisters From Boston"** [Kathryn Grayson, Lauritz Melchoir, Jimmy Durante, Peter Lawford].   [7 weeks to departure!]

July 27   Saturday, (19 months!), I went to Tokyo as usual. Larry and Porter came over and we picked up "Totsi" and took a ride around town. I played Solitaire and saw a show **"Just Before Dawn"** [Warner Baxter, Adele Roberts, Martin Kosleck].

July 28   Sunday, I went to church this morning and in the afternoon, Bob & I went to the beach at Kamakura and went in swimming. The waves were huge and we had a lot of fun.

July 29   Monday, I went to Tokyo as usual and drove around. I looked at some cameras and came back and stayed in tonight.

July 30   Tuesday, I went to Tokyo again looking at cameras. I found a pretty nice one. I came back and it started raining. Farmer & I bought a Coke from Yoshito over at our NCO Club. We saw a show in the Recreation Hall **"Mask of Diijon"** [Erich von Stroheim, Jeanne Bates, William Wright].

July 31   Wednesday, I drove to Tokyo again in rainy weather. I didn't do much. I bought a Mamiya Six III camera for 2950 Yen or almost $200 dollars. It actually cost me $7. [the price in June 1946 was 5,000-10,000 Yen, or $333-$666. I am unsure how Dad got it for $7].

Mamiya Six II camera

1946-08-01 B-29's over Tokyo

1946-08-01 Army Day Parade Eisenhower in front of McArthur's GHq [x] and Emporer's Palace moat, Tokyo

1946-08-01 B-29's peacefully over Tokyo

1946-08-01 Victory Parade

August 1	Thursday, I went to Tokyo again. There was still no unusual occurrence.
August 2	Friday, I went to Tokyo in the pouring down rain today. I came back and Mrs. McClelland came and lied to Mr. Ricarrdi and took my car to Tokyo! [6 weeks to departure!]
August 3	Saturday, Mr. Ricarrdi & Farmer really told Mrs. McClelland off. It sure does my heart proud. Bob & I went to a show and saw **"Wife of Monte Cristo"** [John Loder, Lenore Aubert, Charles Dingle].
August 4	Sunday, I went to church this morning. The Chaplain was off the **"Ainsworth"** ship and delivered the sermon. Then in the afternoon Bob & I took a 2½ ton PMC to Kamakura with an ARC sightseeing tour. We saw all the high Buddha statues and came back to the Recreation Hall and saw **"The Gentlemen Misbehaves"** [Bob Haymes, Osa Massen, Hillary Brooke].
August 5	Monday, I went to Tokyo again and nothing unusual happened. I came back with 4 girls. The radiator is leaking again. I stayed in at night and played Solitaire.
August 6	Tuesday, I got up for Reveille. The mosquitoes ate me all night. I ate chow, then went to Tokyo in the Mercury. I came back over to the hut and ate. Then Bob & I went to see Gene Tierney and Cornel Wilde, Jeanne Crain in **"Leave Her to Heaven."**
August 7	Wednesday, I went to Tokyo again and picked up "Totsi" after dinner and went to the Art Gallery and took a roll of film of her. Then I took her home. I came back at night and met "Mickey" up near the Grand Cherry. She sure is a cute one!
August 8	Thursday, I went to Tokyo as usual today. There was nothing much unusual that happened. I came back and after chow we had a row with the colored soldiers outside our fence. I sure don't like these.
August 9	Friday, I went to Tokyo again today and drove around. I got my pictures, etc. and came back and made another trip to Tokyo after Miss Brindel. I brought her back and rode around awhile. I came in a played Solitaire under my mosquito net and went to sleep. [5 weeks to departure!]
August 10	Saturday, I went to Tokyo this morning. Bob hit a Jap on a bicycle. We drove a Chinese girl to the War Ministry Building. Bob & I ate and came back and saw a **USO** show **"Petticoat Fever"** [Robert Montgomery, Myrna Loy, Reginald Owen].
August 11	Sunday, I went to church this morning. I am just about to give up. We ate dinner and Bob & I drove to Kamakura. The truck got hot and Bob put water in it a lot.
August 12	Monday, today I am 21 years old, a heck of a way to spend a birthday. I drove to Tokyo as usual. It sure is hot. I came back in the afternoon and Bob & I went to a show at night and saw **"Suspense"** [?].
August 13	Tuesday, I went to Tokyo as usual. There is not much doing. I ran around with "Totsi" at noon and took her to work and then came back. Bob & I went on to bed.
August 14	Wednesday, I went to Tokyo again as usual today. It is the First Anniversary of the Surrender of the Japanese. Nothing unusual occurred. Farmer, Bob & I saw a show **"Boys Ranch."** It was a good show.
August 15	Thursday, I went to Tokyo as usual today. Porter went with me today and we looked around Tokyo. I ate and came back to Yokohama. Bob & I saw a **USO** show **"Rhythm Roundup"** at the Octagon Theatre.
August 16	Friday, I went to Tokyo today. "Totsi" wore a bare midriff today. It sure was nice. We went out and took some more pictures today. Bob & I saw a show at night [?].
	[4 weeks to departure!]
August 17	Saturday, Bob & I took a Jeep to Tokyo this morning. We bought 2 cameras and came back and fooled around. Then I went to bed.

1946-08-01 Victory Parade

1946-10 Hiroshima +1 year

1947 Tojo & other war criminals on the way to trials

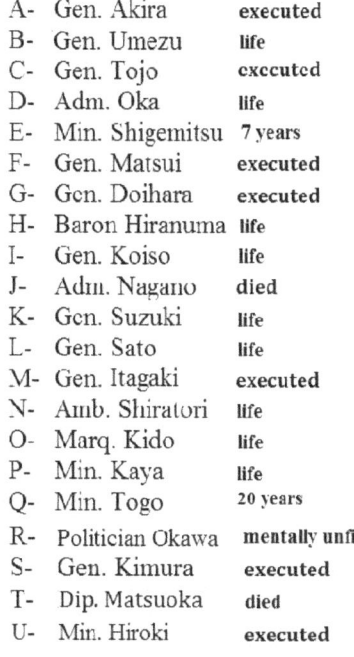

A-	Gen. Akira	executed
B-	Gen. Umezu	life
C-	Gen. Tojo	executed
D-	Adm. Oka	life
E-	Min. Shigemitsu	7 years
F-	Gen. Matsui	executed
G-	Gen. Doihara	executed
H-	Baron Hiranuma	life
I-	Gen. Koiso	life
J-	Adm. Nagano	died
K-	Gen. Suzuki	life
L-	Gen. Sato	life
M-	Gen. Itagaki	executed
N-	Amb. Shiratori	life
O-	Marq. Kido	life
P-	Min. Kaya	life
Q-	Min. Togo	20 years
R-	Politician Okawa	mentally unfit
S-	Gen. Kimura	executed
T-	Dip. Matsuoka	died
U-	Min. Hiroki	executed

Front row of defendants from left to right: Gen. Kenji Doihara; Field Marshal Shunroku Hata; Koki Hirota, former Prime Min. of Japan; Gen. Jiro Minami; Gen. Hideki Tojo, former Prime Min. of Japan; Marine Min. Takasumi Oka; Gen. Yoshijiro Umezu; Gen. Sadao Araki; Gen. Akira Muto; Politician Naoki Hoshino; Fin. Min. Okinori Kaya; Marquis Koichi Kido.
Yasushi Kimura, civilian POW guard; Back row: Colonel
Kingiro Hashimoto; Gen. Kuniaki Koiso; Adm. Osami Nagano; Gen. Hiroshi Oshima; Gen. Iwane Matsui; Nationalist Shumei Okawa; Baron Kiichiro Hiranuma; Foreign Min. Shigenori Togo; Foreign Min. Yosuke Matsuoka; Foreign Min. Mamoru Shigemitsu; Gen. Kenryo Sato; Adm. Shigetaro Shimada; Ambassador Toshio Shiratori; Gen. Teiichi Suzuki., Gen. Seishiro Itagaki, designer over Asian POW camps.

(L-R) General Tojo , premier at time of Pear Harbor; Adm. Oka (navy ex-bureau chief); General Umezu, ex-chief of general staff; General Arak

In this photo: Sadao Araki, Akira Muto, Takasumi Oka, Shumei Okawa, Hideki Tojo, Yoshijiro Umezu

Mt. Fuji 1982 eruption

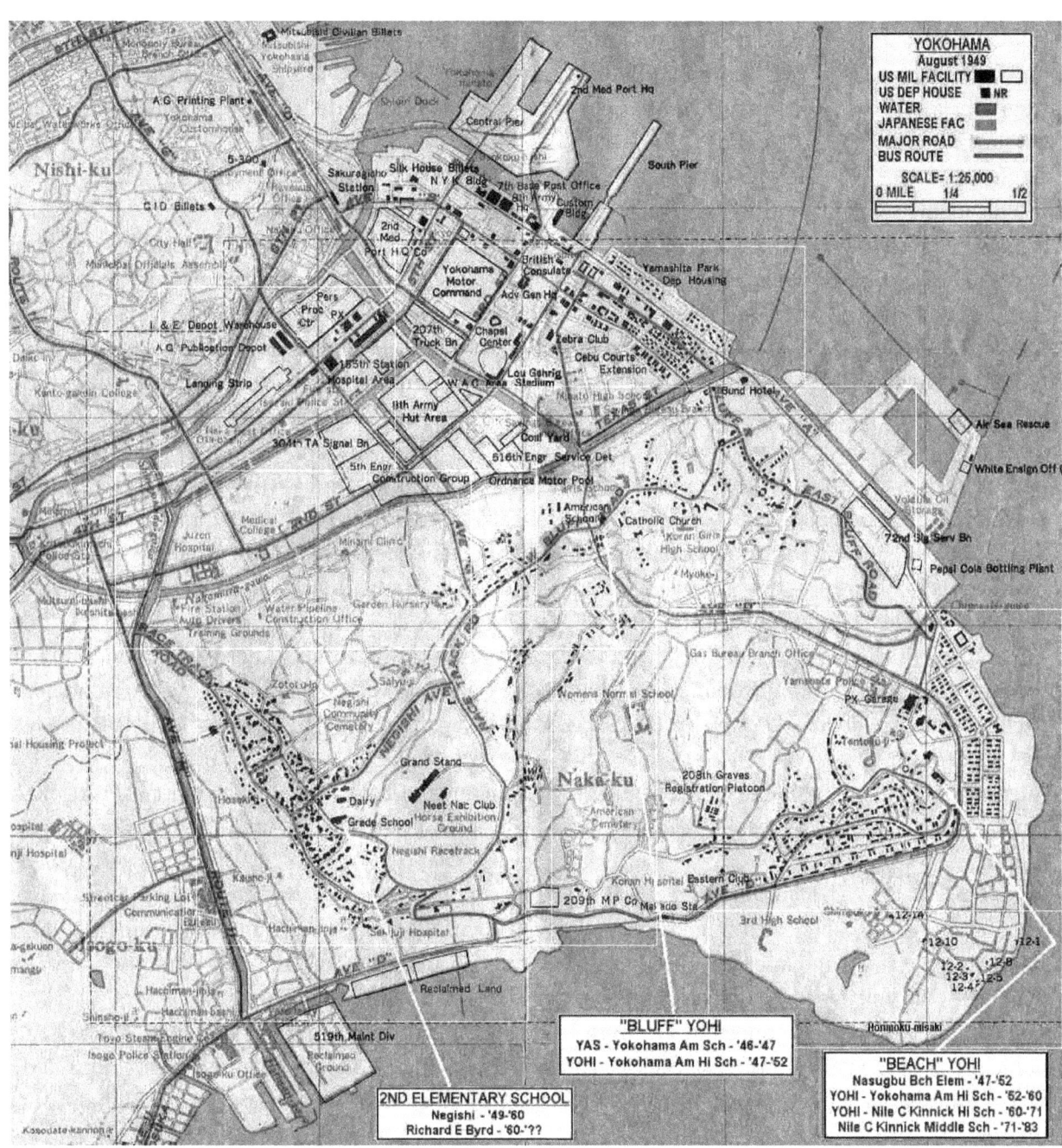

1949 City Map of Yokohama Japan

August 18 Sunday, I went to church in the morning and lay around the hut all afternoon and night. Bob & I saw **"Joe Palooka, Champ"** [Leon Errol, Joe Kirkwood, Jr., Elyse Know].

August 19 Monday, I went to Tokyo as usual and didn't do hardly anything. I came back and lay around the hut all night.

August 20 Tuesday, I went to Tokyo as usual today, but nothing unusual. Today, new replacements came in and I went out and rode around with one of them.

August 21 Wednesday, I went to Tokyo today, but nothing unusual up there. I came back and had Ruth's Jeep. Hodge, Bob & I drove around and saw Mickey. We went to a show **"It Shouldn't Happen to a Dog"** [Carole Landis, Allyn Joslyn, Margo Woode].

August 22 Thursday, I went to Tokyo. It was a rather dull day. I saw a fire in a 8 story Jap building. The Jap and GI fire trucks were both there for a couple of hours. I saw Mickey at night. She is sure a cute little girl.

August 23 Friday, I went to Tokyo as usual. Today was quite uneventful. I came back and found a nice place, Cabarat. Hodge & I looked around and went to a show with Bette Davis entitled **"A Stolen Life"** [Glenn Ford, Dana Clark].   [3 weeks to departure]

August 24 Saturday, I took the Jeep to Tokyo and did nothing but run around and shop. I took 2 girls back and went to Sakura Park Caberat and met "Madrir Marie," a little waitress 17 years old, a young fresh beauty. She sure is cute.

August 25 Sunday, Hodge and I went to church this morning. There was a good sermon. In the afternoon we went to Enoshima. MP's got my Jeep and we walked out after it but wouldn't get it back. We hitch-hiked back to the hut. I went to Caberat again and talked with Marie till 8:45pm when they closed.

August 26 Monday, I drove the grey ambulance to Tokyo today. The Mercury is broken down. I drove around and came back with 7 girls. Hodge & I went to Caberat and saw "Marie" again tonight. She sure is cute!

August 27 Tuesday, I went to Tokyo again, still driving the grey ambulance. I took Miss Todd to the 42nd Hospital and came back and played Hearts. After chow Hodge and I went to Caberat. "Marie" and I talked and later I walked her to the train station. She says 'only one Kaebita.' Maybe so, maybe not we will ever see. She is a very nice girl.

August 28 Wednesday, I went to Tokyo again, but nothing much happened. I took "Totsi" home. She wore a yellow-greenish dress. I came back and then Hodge & I went to the Caberat and show **"Muddy."** Then we went to the show and saw **"Devil's Mark"** [Anita Louise, Jim Bannon, Michael Duane].

August 29 Thursday, I went to Tokyo again today and drove around and then came back with Miss Nadeau. After chow and at 5:30 Inspection, Hodge & I went to Tokyo and looked for "Totsi" and finally went to Ernie Pyle and saw an Australian **USO** show. I went to the snack bar and then back to Yokohama.

August 30 Friday, I went to Tokyo as usual. Today there was nothing unusual. Larry and I took "Totsi" for a ride in the ambulance and came back. There is a broken spring and spring bolt on the ambulance. After supper, Hodge and I saw **"Night Editor"** [William Gargan, Janis Carter, Jeff Donnell].
[2 weeks to departure!]

August 31 Saturday, I went to Tokyo today and drove the Station Wagon up there. I came Back and Hodge and I saw a show **"Gilda."** [Rita Hayworth, Glenn Ford, George Macready]

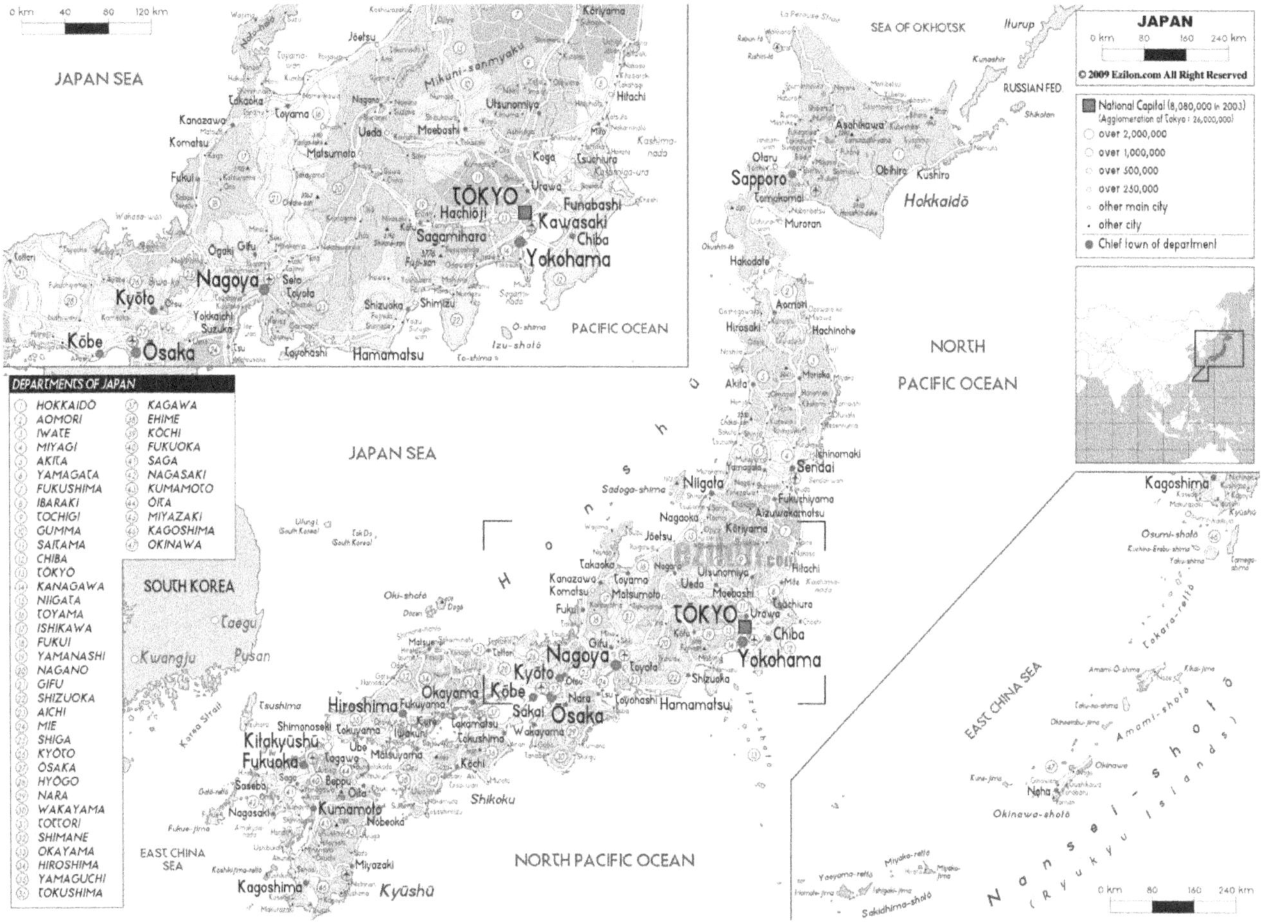

Yokohama National War Cemetery

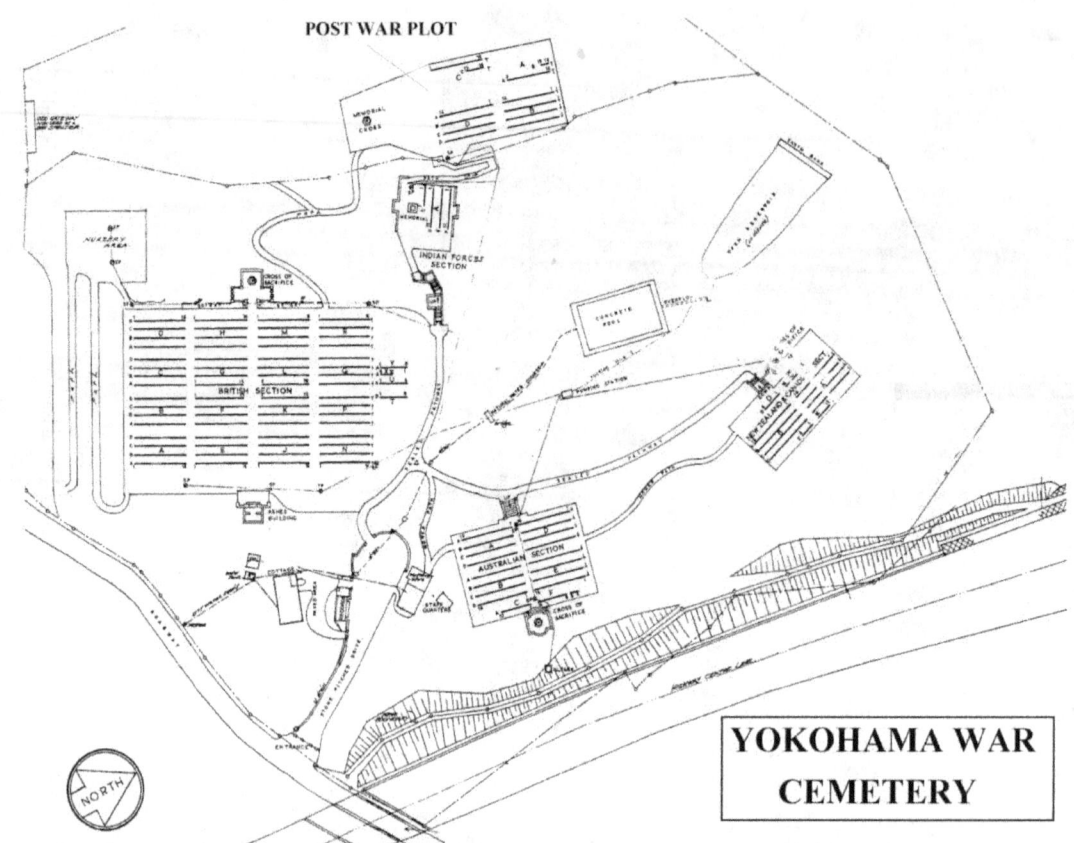

Yokohama today

Scenes of Yokohama today

Mount Fujiyama today

September 1   Sunday, I went to church this morning and in the afternoon Hodge & I went to Enoshima in the afternoon. We went rowing and met "Millie," a Portuguese girl. I saw the show **"The Strange Triangle."** [Signe Hasso, Preston Foster, Anabel Shaw]

September 2   Monday, Hodge & I bought some new binoculars and were up at the swimming pool watching the girls with our glasses. I saw a show **"Anna and the King of Siam."** [Irene Dunne, Rex Harrison, Linda Darnell]

September 3   Tuesday, I went to Tokyo again today and saw Ruth and Farmer. I put in my order for a small camera. I ate chow, came back and Hodge & I drove around and started to see a show, but came back and went to bed.

September 4   Wednesday, I went to Tokyo today and drove around, but didn't do much. I picked up a cute **USO** girl, ate lunch and came back. "Cotton" and I went to a show and got behind 2 girls—cute!

September 5   Thursday, I went to Tokyo and it was quite dead today. I came looking after a PFC Euitah (T5)—Hodge & I saw a show **"The Bandit of Sherwood Forest."** [Anita Louis, Jill Esmond, Edgar Buchanan]

September 6   Friday, I went to Tokyo as usual and picked up "Totsi" and then came back.
        [1 week until departure!]

September 7   Saturday, I went to Tokyo for the **LAST TIME** today I guess. I hurried back to the [hut] area.

September 8   Sunday, I went to church in the morning. After PT clearance sheet I started to dous with sections. I went to a show at night.

September 9   Monday, I just lay around today and got a couple shots.

September 10   Tuesday, After recruiting till 12:30pm, I finally got our orders and went to the 4th Regimental Depot about 2:30pm. They say we should ship out Wednesday.

September 11   Wednesday, I lay around all day and was processed at 9 o'clock at night.

September 12   Thursday, So far, I just lay in bed all day (1:15pm). George, John, Deffie and Oliver left [for home].

September 13   Friday, I got on the ship "Norway [Victory]." We didn't sail until Sunday morning though.

1946-09 Norway Victory- from Yokasuka, Japan to Seattle, WA

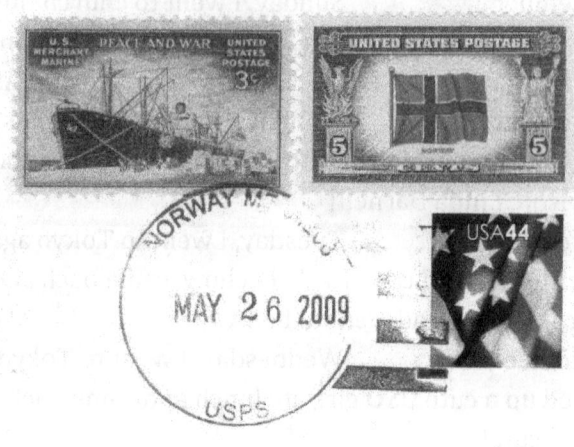

World War II Victory Ships Named for Allied Nations

SS NORWAY VICTORY

Named for the Kingdom of Norway
Launched on February 12, 1944 by
Oregon Shipbuilding Corp.
Portland, Oregon

Commemorative USPC Card from 2009

[#89, SS Norway Victory, VC2-S-AP3, Keel Laid: 12/17/1943, Launched: 2/12/1944, Delivered: 3/31/1944].

9/13/1946 Dad on board the "Norway Victory" ship- Yokasuka, Japan to Seattle, WA

[September 14]	*[Saturday, waiting on ship]*
[September 15]	*[Sunday, set sail at noon. It stormed later]*
[September 16]	*[Monday, It stormed all day.]*
[September 17]	*[Tuesday, It stormed all day.]*
[September 18]	*[Wednesday, It stormed all day.]*

I was never so sick in all my life. You are just being tossed around like a bobble.

[September 19]	Thursday, I began eating a little and we crossed the International Date Line.
[September 20]	*[Friday]*
[September 21]	*[Saturday]* Today is Saturday.

September 22	Sunday, I stayed on the ship deck sleeping and daydreaming at night. I became extremely depressed a couple of times.

[September 23]	Monday, I just slept and ate soup and daydreamed.

[September 24]	Tuesday, I just slept and ate soup and daydreamed.

[September 25]	Wednesday, I just slept and ate soup and daydreamed. We saw land Wednesday night and lights!

[September 26]	Thursday morning we docked at Seattle [, WA]. There was a **USO** show to greet us at the pier. What a wonderful feeling riding to Ft. Lawton. I was impressed by thousands of autos. At Ft. Lawton Jack Snead and I went to the PX. We were overwhelmed and bought a Parker 51 pen, ice cream and milk. We ate steak and saw a show **"Three Little Girls in Blue"** at night. [June Haver, George Montgomery, Vivian Blaine]. These were the best days I've ever spent. I went out to dance at the singing club.

September 27	Friday, I loaded my baggage on the train and left Seattle about 1:30 in the afternoon. Everything is mountain, mountains and all.

September 28	Saturday, I got the jeep in Montana and ate dinner and a shower. We stopped in Missoula and got off the train. Cute girls were in the town and looked good.

September 29	Sunday, I travelled across to Lincoln, NB and ate some swell eggs in the morning.

September 30	Monday, I went across Nebraska, Iowa, Minnesota and Chicago on Monday.

October 1	Tuesday, I woke up near Fostoria, Ohio in the morning and got to Washington, DC night. I called Gloria in Washington. It sure was good to talk to her.

[October 2]	Wednesday morning we arrived at Ft. Bragg, NC and started reparation processing. It went on for days.

[October 3]	*Thursday, [reparation processing]*
[October 4]	*Friday, [reparation processing]*
[October 5]	*Saturday, [reparation processing]*
[October 6]	*Sunday, [reparation processing].*

Hank & I went to Fayetteville and ate dinner and came back. Get a 46-day furlough tomorrow.

October 7	Monday, I went around and waited for papers till the afternoon. I left in a taxi to Sanford and on a bus to Charlotte, where Mom & Dad & Don met me at 10:30pm. Betty has a girl named "Carol Ann."

"The Page of Pages" October 7, 1946, my 46-day Terminal Leave begins. I was discharged November 22, 1946 at Fort Bragg, North Carolina, as a Corporal Technician 5th Grade.

[The End]

Movies & Movie Posters- Films that John saw in Japan

- "Abilene Town"
- "Along Came Jones"
- "Anna and the King of Siam"
- "Bad Girls"
- "Bedside Manner"
- "Behind the Green Lights"
- "Captain Kidd"
- "China Sky"
- "Cinderella Jones"
- "Colonel Effingham's Raid"
- "Cornered"
- "Diamond Horseshoe"
- "Don Juan Quilligan"
- "Dragon Seed"
- "Dragonwyck"
- "Gilda"
- "Her Highness and the Bellboy"
- "Here Come the Co-eds"
- "Hold That Blonde"
- "In This Our Life" [1942]
- "Johnny Angel"
- "Keys of the Kingdom"
- "Kiss and Tell"
- "Leave Her to Heaven"
- "Life with Blondie"
- "Little Giant"
- "Our Vines Have Tender Grapes"
- "Panama Hattie"
- "Practically Yours"
- "Rhapsody in Blue"
- "Salome, Where She Danced"
- "San Antonio"
- "Saratoga Trunk"
- "Scared Stiff"
- "Scarlet Street"
- "Southern"
- "Spellbound"
- "State Fair"
- "Summer Storm"
- "Swing Parade of 1946"
- "Tars & Spars"
- "Tarzan and the Green Goddess"
- "Ten Cents a Dance"
- "The ABC's of the USA"
- "The Bandit of Sherwood Forest"
- "The Big Sleep"
- "The Blue Dahlia"
- "The Body Snatcher"
- "The Dark Corner"
- "The Dolly Sisters"
- "The Harvey Girls"
- "The Mask of Diljon"
- "The Postman Always Rings Twice"
- "The Sailor takes a Wife"
- "The Spiral Staircase"
- "The Stork Club"
- "The Valley of Decision"
- "The Wife of Monte Cristo"
- "They Were Expendable"
- "Thrill of a Romance"
- "Tin Pan Alley"
- "Two Sisters From Boston"
- "Unashamed"
- "Under the Sun"
- "Up Goes Maisie"
- "Weekend Pass"
- "Week-end at the Waldorf"
- "Wilson"
- "Within These Walls"
- "Ziegfeld Follies"

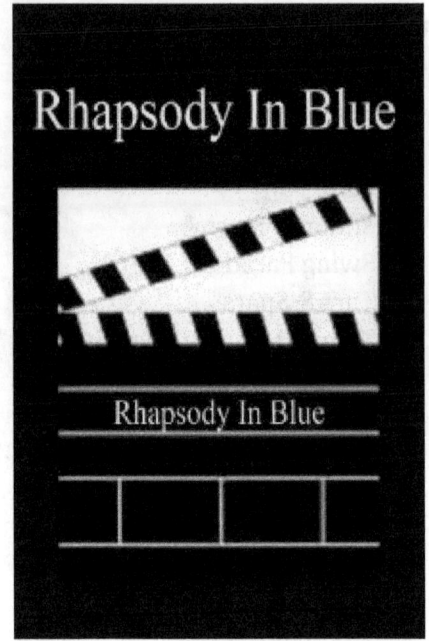
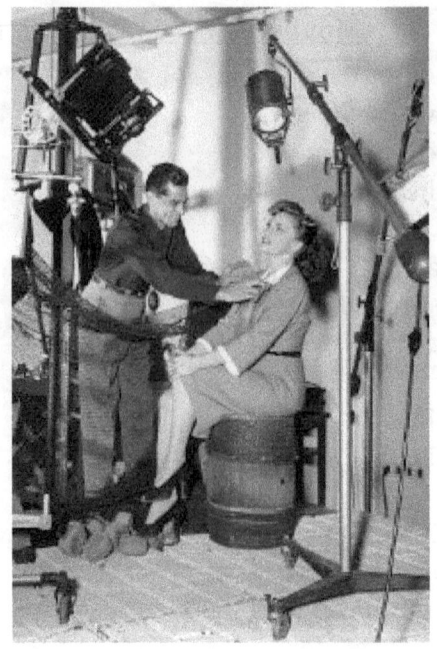

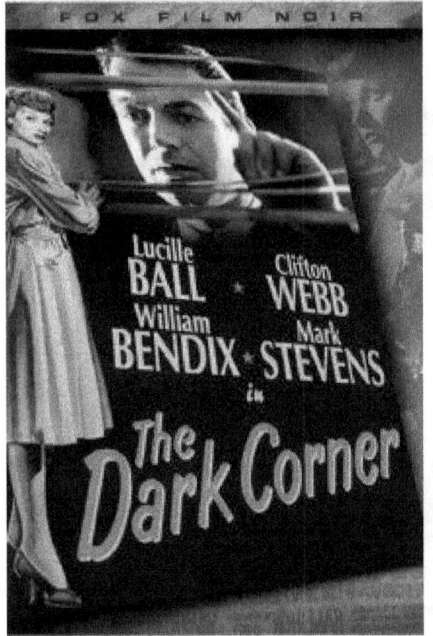

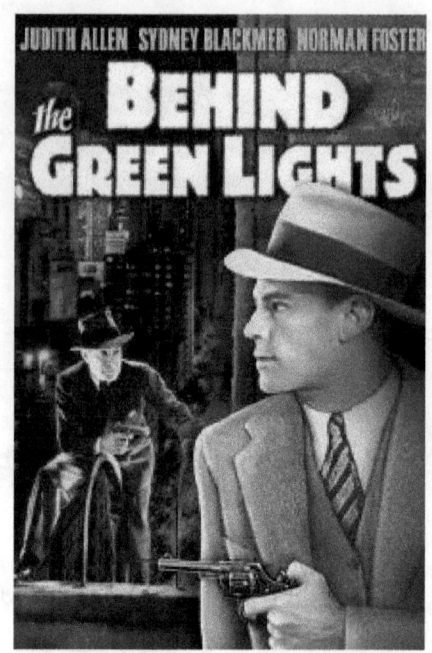

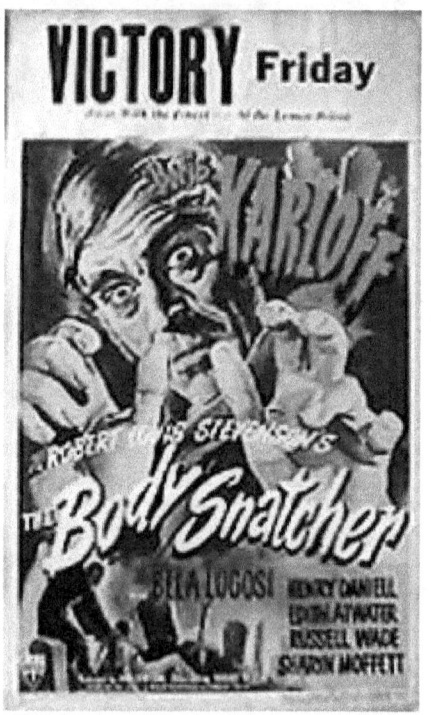

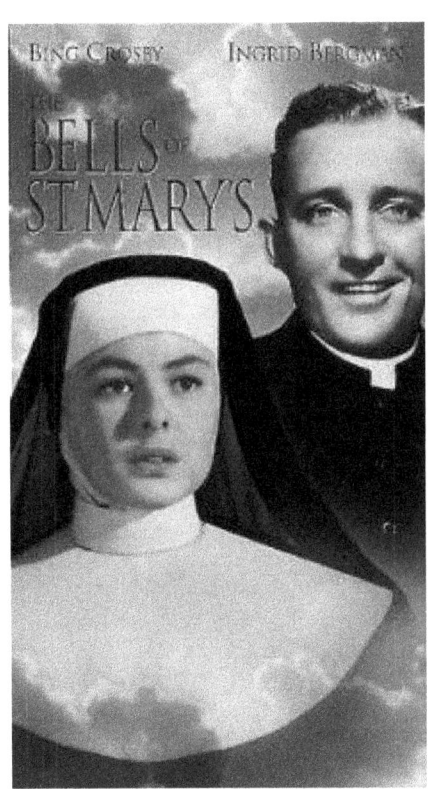

Chapter 7: Merrell Berniece Mull

The old Huffman house where Bernie lived [above] and the complex family chart [below] of Marvin Mull {left column} and Peggy Huffman {right column}

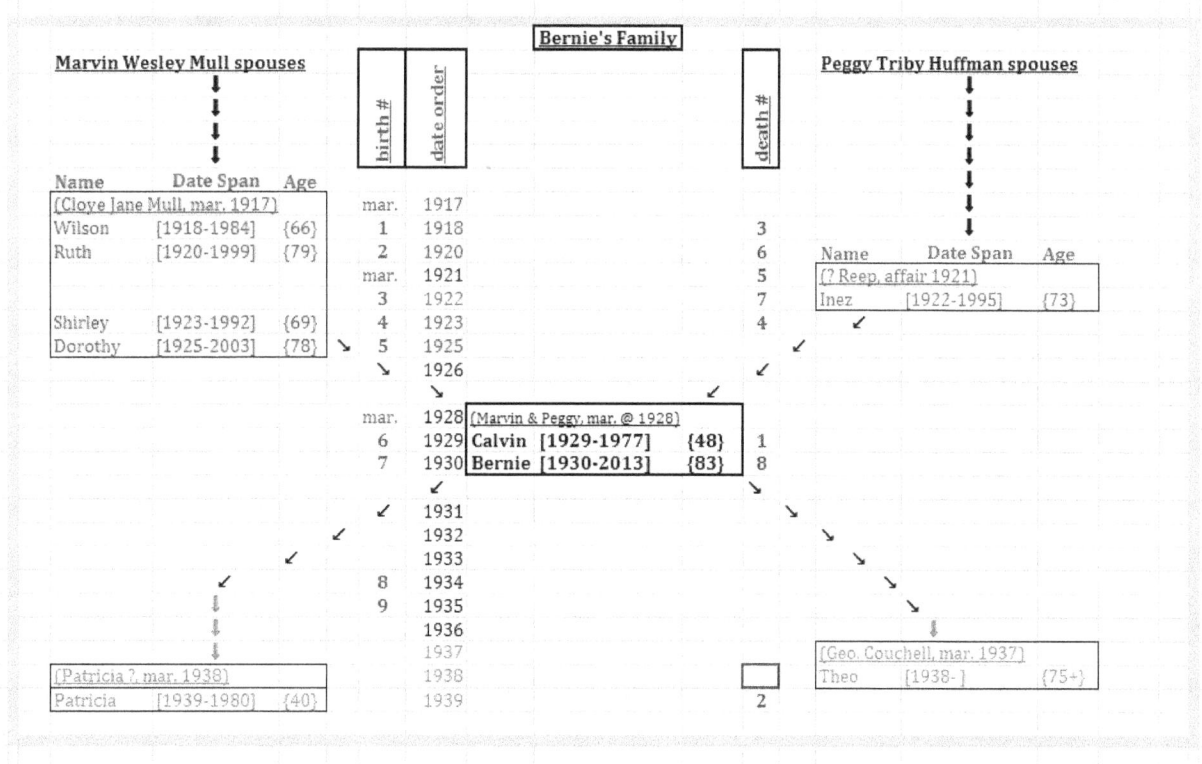

Calvin and Berneice at the Methodist Children's Home in Winston-Salem, NC

Bernie and Calvin- 1937 at the Children's Home

Bernie and Calvin on the steps of the Administration Building

Bernie & Calvin with Ruth, Peggy & Shirley - 1937 at the Home

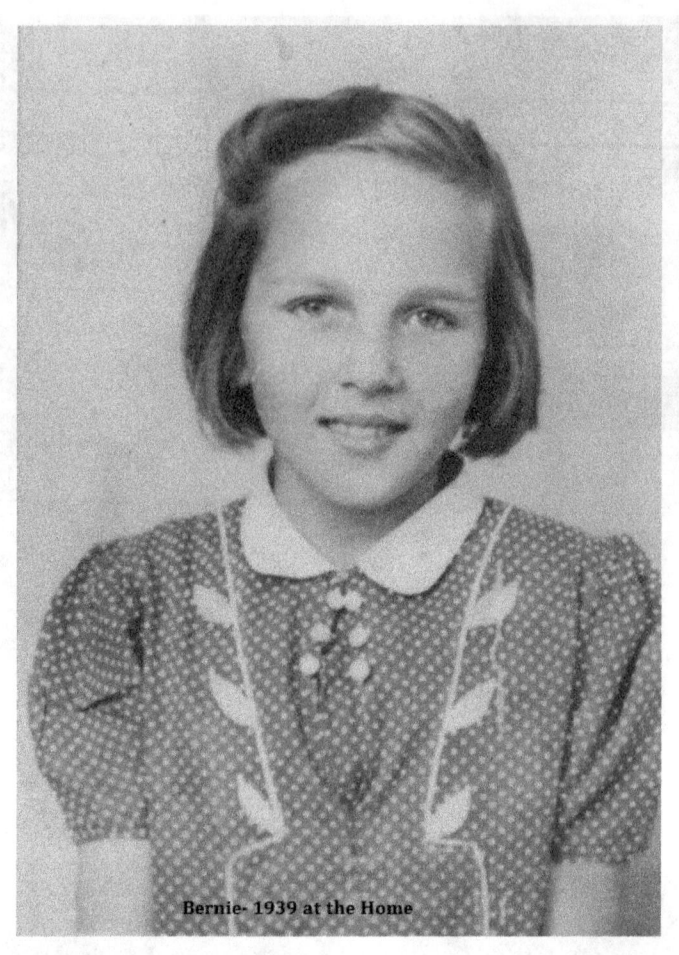

Bernie- 1939 at the Home

Bernie was at the Methodist Children's Home in Winston-Salem from 1934-1945 with her only full sibling: Calvin.
They received visits from the family, but it was not the same as living at home.
[left]

[below]:
Her grandfather's store, next to the Morganton Cemetery. It was later handed down to H.J. Mull.

Bernie, Calvin and little Judy Ratledge in Charlotte

Chapter 8: John & Bernie after the War

1947- Bernie at Sharon Memorial Park, Charlotte

With John Carriker's new post-war car: a 1941 creamy yellow Chevy with red interior!

John and Don in 1947 at Indian Trail PC Manse

John in the manse at Indian Trail Presbyterian Church, NC

John at Carolina Beach, NC in 1947. Note the trolley wires

Richard & Nancy Gordon and John Carriker & Bernie Mull
in summer 1948 on Lake Wylie below Buster Boyd Bridge on US #49

Jack & Bernie at Lake Wylie, summer 1948

John at the Eastminster PC Manse on Monroe Rd., dressed for Dorothy Jane's wedding in 1948

Various shots of Bernie on a picnic with John

Bernie at Bat Cave, NC- 1948

Bat Cave 1948

Bernie at Latta Park in 1948

Latta Park in 1948

early 1948 portrait of Bernie

Dad's favorite photo of mom!

Another school photograph

Norma, Calvin and Bernie at Latta Park, Charlotte

The Reverend John A. Carriker moved from Eldorado, Texas back to the old North State in 1946 and had a shared ministry at Indian Trail Presbyterian Church and Siler Presbyterian Church [in Wesley Chapel]. The family lived in the manse of the Indian Trail church.

Siler Presbyterian Church

Chapter 9: A New Family

Big snow of Dec. 1951 on Shenandoah Ave.

1953 snow at Eastminster PC, Charlotte, NC

Bernie- Dec. 1953
23 after 4 children!

John Jr., 1955

John & Bernie 1956

Betty & Bernie, July 1956

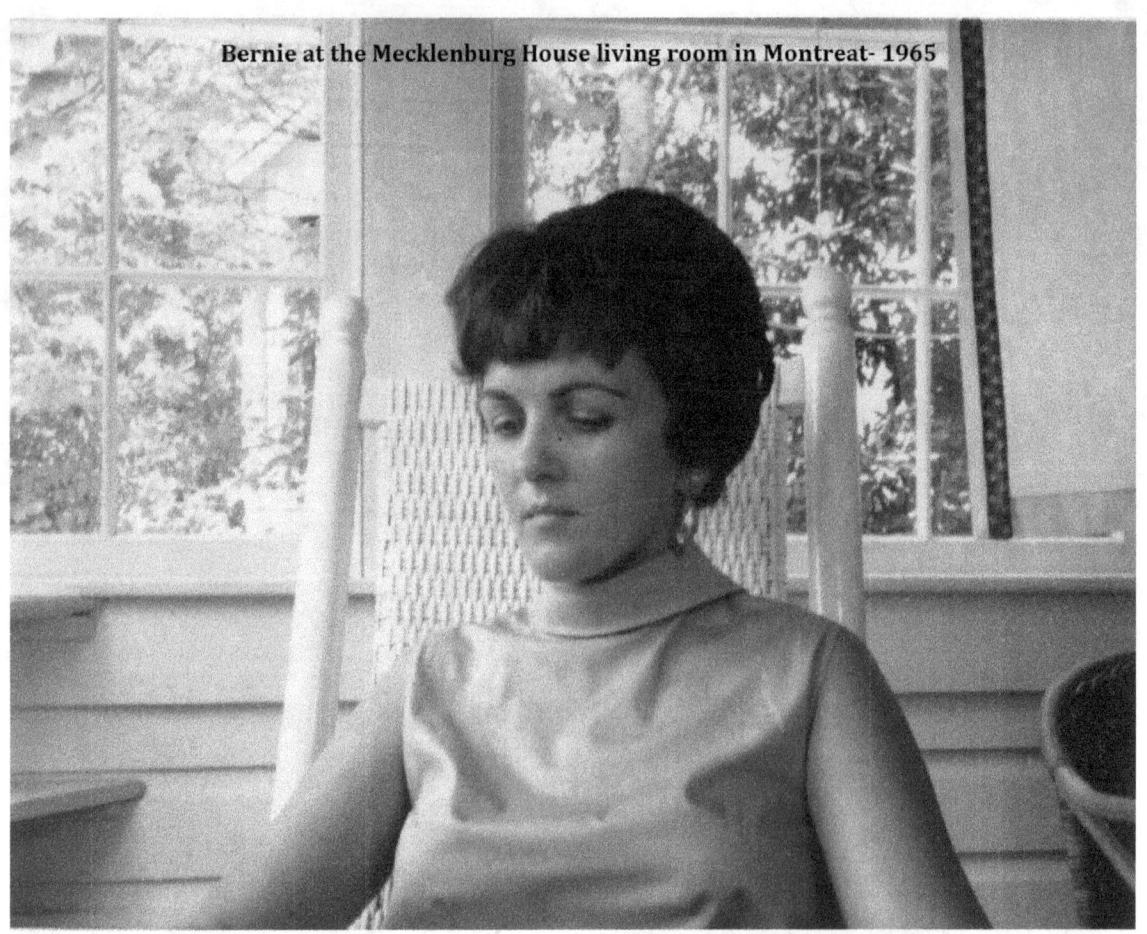
Bernie at the Mecklenburg House living room in Montreat- 1965

Children of Marvin Wesley Mull at his funeral in 1966:
[by Cloye]: Ruth, Wilson, Shirley, Calvin [by Peggy], Dorothy [Cloye] and Bernie [Peggy]

The Mecklenburg House on Texas Road Extension in Montreat. It was demolished after 2001.

234

Chapter 10: Four Little Boys

Carol and John 3rd
1949

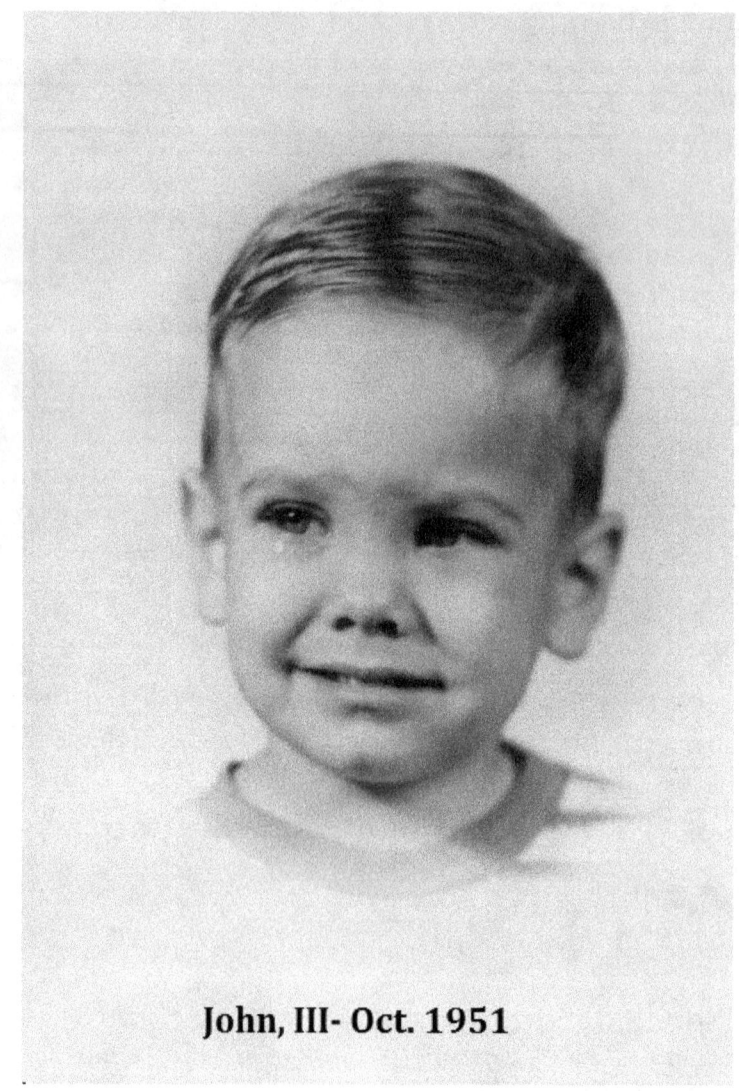

John, III- Oct. 1951

Poor little John, on receiving news he is not an only child!
I was born just 3 months prior to this photograph.

The car in the background is Dad's 3rd car, a 1947 light green Pontiac, with wheel skirts!

Eastminster PC, Charlotte- Mar. 1953: frt- Ed, Carol, Laura, David, John III; mid- Annie, Betsy, John Jr., Bernie, Dorothy Jane, Wayne; back- Alpha Jr., John Sr.

Sept. 24, 1952 in Elizaville, KY at the Dorsey house

Mampaw [90½], David [14 mo.], Bernie [21¾], John III [38 mo.], Ella [61]

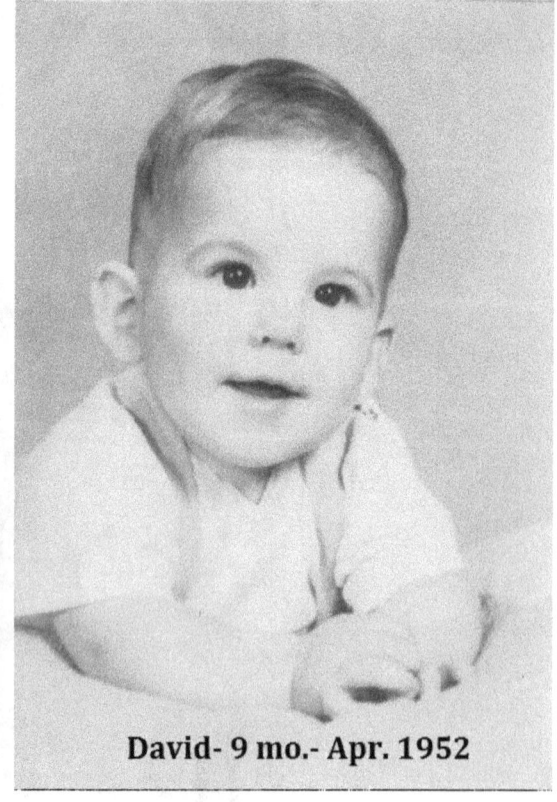

David- 9 mo.- Apr. 1952

Myrtle Beach, SC- July 1954
David, Betsy, Timmy, John III, Bernie, John Jr.

Jan. 1955 big snow
John III holding Richard, Tim, David

Our homemade Easter Suits- 1957 at Eastminster Presbyterian, Charlotte

Sept. 1959- John & Betsy Carriker with friends at Assembly Inn in Montreat

The Carrikers first camper... a Rod 'n Reel 16-footer at Myrtle Beach State Park!
John takes the photo while everyone waves to the camera as we head home.
The car is a 1960 Pontiac wagon.

Bernie & John Jr., John Sr. & Betsy and Don, with [frt.] Richard, Tim, David and John III- Feb. 1958 at Eastminster Presbyterian Church, Chipley Ave., Charlotte, NC

Tim at Myrtle Beach in 1956, before we started camping

Little Tim in 1956 in his pajamas on a spring day.

Richard is standing outside of Eastminster Presbyterian Church, located behind the old Ovens Auditorium, taken about 1956.

Trailer #2: an 18-foot Nomad [for 6 people!]. Those two extra feet made a difference. The car is our short-lived 1960 Rambler when camped at Myrtle Beach State Park.

The Nomad and Rambler again.

Bernie at Myrtle Beach State Park, June 1963

One of our Jungle Hammocks at a campsite at Lakewood Family Campground in 1963.

by the house on Winterfield in Sept. 1967- David, Richard, Bernie, Tim & John III

a snowy backyard on Winterfield Pl., Charlotte- 1968

Dad's new Allis-Chalmers tractor with a snow-blade and rear-tire chains in 1968

John and Bernie Carriker in 1968

Key West, FL - Feb. 20, 1969, preparing to head home 890 miles away.

Chapter 11: More Little Boys... and Girls! The Grandchildren

Bernie's first grandchild: John Anderson Carriker, IV

John IV and his mother, Sandy Crump Carriker

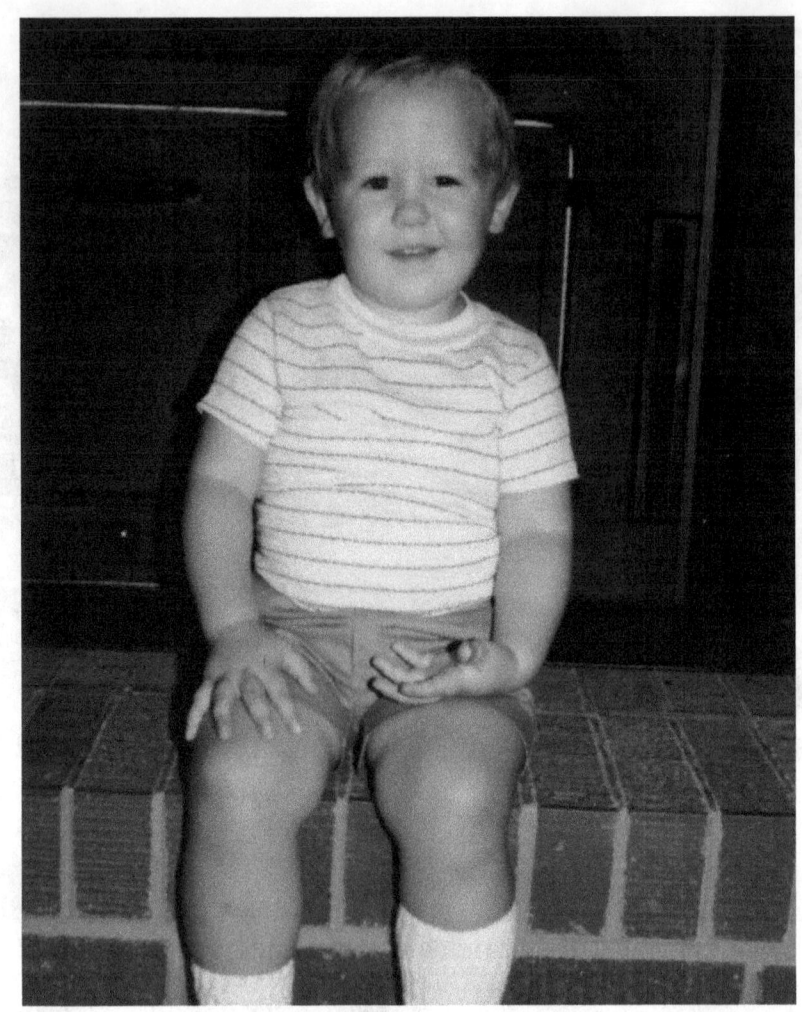

Samuel David Carriker, Jr.
[also known as Little David, Davy and Dave]

Dave and John IV at Clingmans Dome. They were good travel buddies!

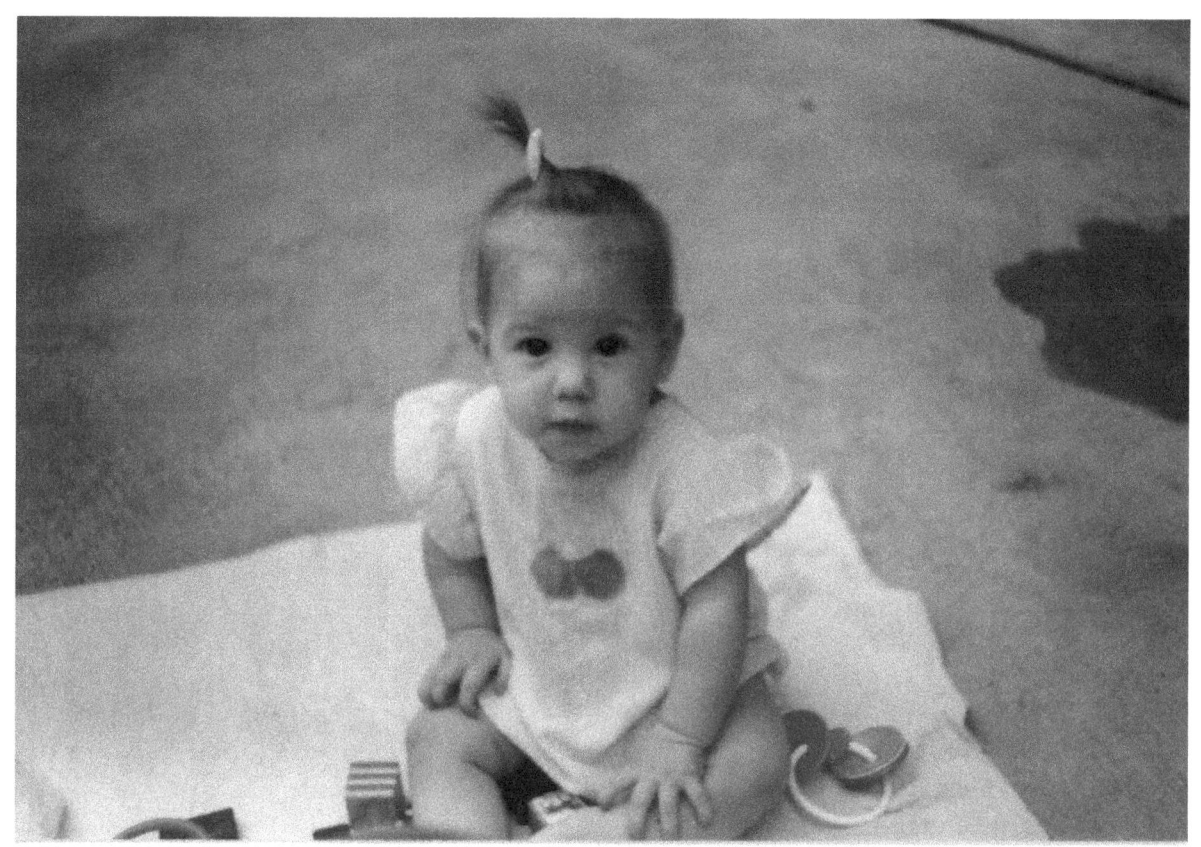
Baby Ashleigh is David's second child, seen at Granddaddy John's in 1981.

Ashleigh's best friend in childhood was Jenny Nelson! She went with us everywhere!

Jonathan was David's third child, showing off his new turkey hat that he received from his other grandparents: Dave & Elsie Covington, who owned a turkey farm.

First Day of School for Jonathan!

Rebekah was David's fourth child, giving a hug to Granddaddy John!

A few years after Rebekah was born, little Joseph Paul Carriker was born dead after nine months and 3 days of gestation. He received his last checkup three days earlier and everything seemed alright. In rolling in the womb he inadvertently tied a knot in his umbilical cord, which deprived him of nourishment and oxygen.

Bekah was three years old when she got on stage with a cowgirl and Chip & Dale, who sang Happy Birthday to her before the audience at the campfire and movie presentation in Fort Wilderness Campground at Walt Disney World, Feb. 14, 1987.

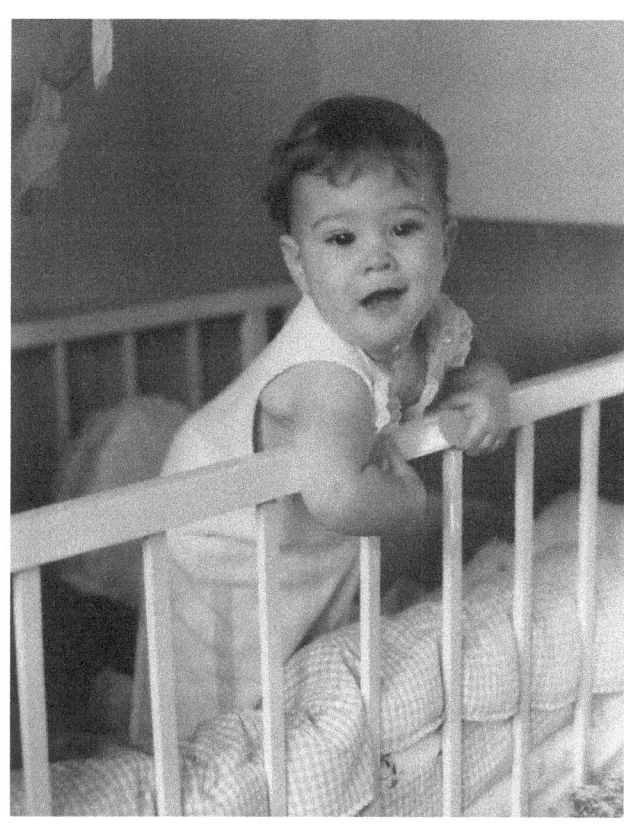

Jenny was the first daughter of Tim & Marta Carriker and is seen in the crib in 1981 [left] and laughing in excitement in 1984 [below]

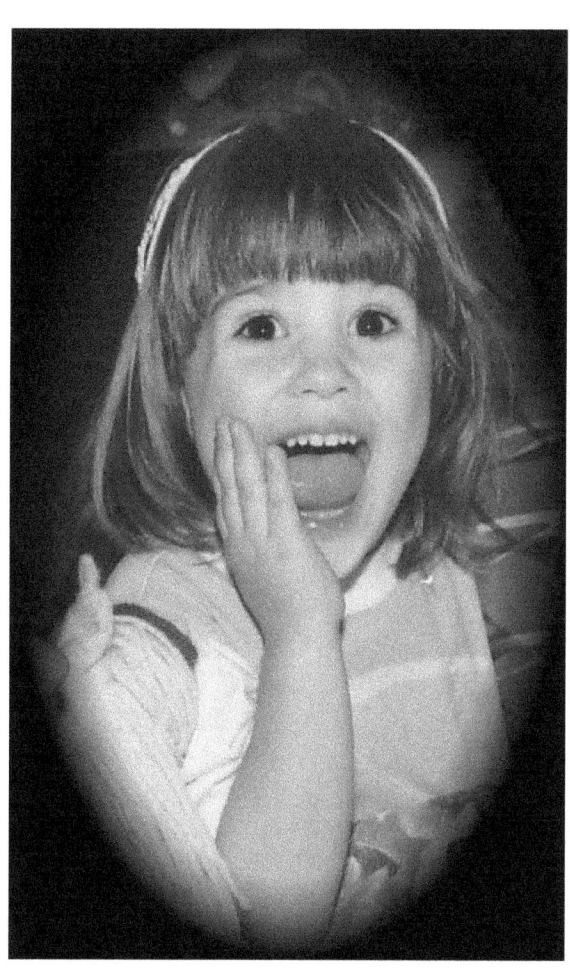

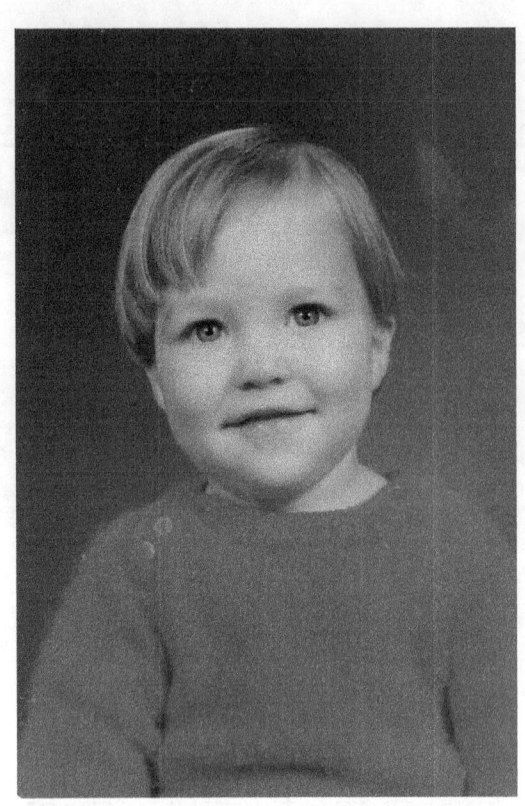

Timmy Jr. was born to Tim & Marta in 1982 and is seen in this 1984 photo [above] and 1986 [below]

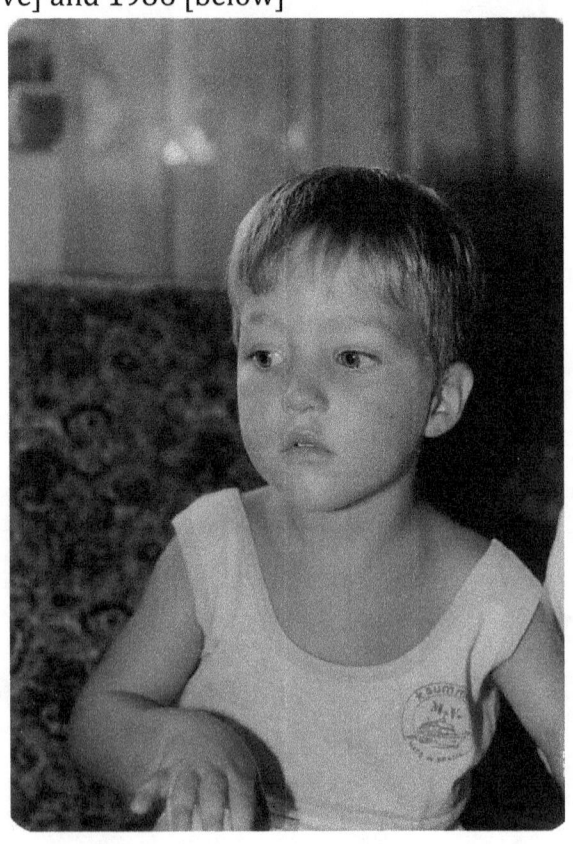

Sarah Kerr Carriker was the third child of Tim & Marta Carriker, being given the maiden name of her mother, 'Kerr' [pronounced *care*]. The Kerr family was from a long line of Presbyterians who went from the United States to Brazil after the Civil War.

Chapter 12: And Great Grandchildren Too!

Jack Adam Carriker [b. 2004] is the son of John Anderson Carriker, IV and Shannan Pully
Carriker, the grandson of John Anderson Carriker, III and Sandy Crump Carriker
and the first great grandson of John & Bernie Carriker.

Jonathan Paul Carriker, [b. 2006] is the son of Jonathan Michael Carriker and Tara Rogers, grandson of Samuel David Carriker, Sr. and Joyce Henry Carriker [Burns] and the second great grandson of John & Bernie Carriker

Hannah Elizabeth Motley [b. 2008] is the daughter of Bekah Carriker & Ben Motley, Grand-daughter of Samuel David Carriker, Sr. and Joyce Henry Carriker [Burns] and the great grand-daughter of John & Bernie Carriker

Anabel Carriker was born 2007 in Hawaii to Tim Carriker, Jr. and Liseth Figeuro and was the first granddaughter of Tim & Marta K. Carriker and the first great granddaughter of John & Bernie Carriker.

Marcelo Carriker [born 2009 in Hawaii] is the grandson of Tim & Marta K. Carriker
And the great grandson of John & Bernie Carriker

Little Gabrielle Kairi Carriker Lauria was born October 8, 2013 in Florianopolis, Brasil
And is the daughter of Michael & Jenny C. Lauria,
The granddaughter of Tim & Marta K. Carriker
And the great granddaughter of John & Bernie Carriker.
She was born the day before her great grandmother went to be with the Lord.

Chapter 13: One Plus One Equals Thirty

Parents
John, Jr. & Bernie =   2

Children
John, III & Sandy +
David [& Joyce] +
Tim & Marta +
Richard   7

Grandchildren
John, IV & Shannan +   2
Dave & Michelle +   2
Ashleigh +   1
Jon [& Tara] & Lauren +   3
Bekah & Ben +   2
Joseph   1
Jenny & Michael +
Timmy [& Lisseth] +
Sarah   3

Great Grandchildren
Jack   1
Jonathan +
Hannah   2
Anabel +
Marcelo   <u>2</u>
Gabrielle   1
                                                    Total   <u>29</u>

John,
You're Not in Kansas Anymore.

You are with your family
and
you are forever loved.

Appendix

The End of World War II in the European Theatre

April 1945	Allied forces begin to take 2.4 million Axis prisoners.
25 April 1945	The last Germans were expelled by the Finnish Army from Finland and retreated into Norway.
27 April 1945	Italian dictator Benito Mussolini was captured by Italian partisans. On 28 April, Mussolini was executed in Giulino.
29 April 1945,	the day before Hitler died, SS General Karl Wolff signed a surrender document at Caserta, Italy for May 2. Nearly 1,000,000 men in Italy and Austria surrendered unconditionally to British General Harold Alexander at 2pm.
30 April 1945	German dictator Adolf Hitler committed suicide in his *Führerbunker* along with Eva Braun at 3:30pm.
1 May 1945	Joseph Goebbels, the new chancellor of Germany for only 29 hours, committed suicide at 8:15pm.
2 May 1945	The Battle of Berlin ended.
4 May 1945	German forces in North West Germany, Denmark, the Netherlands & Bavaria surrender.
6 May 1945	Hermann Göring's surrender.
7 May 1945	President Dönitz ordered Gen. Jodl and Gen. Keitel to surrender all German armed forces unconditionally at 11:01pm.
8 May 1945	Victory in Europe
8 May – 4 September 1945	"German holdout" units cease fire 5/8, 5/9, 5/12, 5/13, 5/15, 5/16, 5/20, 9/4
23 May 1945	President [23 days] Adm. Karl Dönitz's government ordered dissolved by Eisenhower, with Dönitz's arrest at 10:00am.

Major Bombing Sites in World War II

Town	Type	Date	Death-toll	Aircraft	
Dresden	3900 tons- ID	Feb. 13-15, 1944	25,000	360 Lancasters/316 B-17s	[676 large planes]
Tokyo	1700 tons- ID	March 9-10/1945	100,000	279 B-29s	[279 B-29s]
Hiroshima	Ur-235 fission	August 6, 1945	90,000	1 B-29	[1 B-29]
Nagasaki	Pu-240 implosion	August 9, 1945	80,000	1 B-29	[1 B-29]

Final Events in the Asian Theatre of the war

- **Final Events in the Asian Theatre of the war**
- August 3, 1945 – Soviet General Vasilevskii reported to Stalin that Soviet forces ready for invasion from August 7.
- August 6, 1945 – An atomic bomb, Little Boy, dropped on Hiroshima by B-29 *Enola Gay*, flown by Col. Paul Tibbets.
- August 8, 1945 – The Soviet Union declares war on Japan.
- August 9, 1945 – Soviet Armies launch the Soviet invasion of Manchuria.
- August 9, 1945 – Second atomic bomb, Fat Man, is dropped on Nagasaki by B-29 *Bockscar* flown by Maj. Charles Sweeney
- August 9, 1945 – Emperor Hirohito ordered that the Allied terms for the end of the war be accepted.
- August 10, 1945 – The 38th Parallel is set as the delineation between the Soviet and US occupation zones in Korea.
- **August 14, 1945 – Emperor Hirohito's decree to surrender announced over radio.**
- August 14, 1945 – General Douglas MacArthur is appointed to head the occupation forces in Japan.
- August 16, 1945 – Gen. Wainwright, a POW since May 6, 1942, is released from a POW camp in Manchuria.
- August 17, 1945 – Japanese IGHQ issues formal cease-fire in Manchuria.
- August 17, 1945 – General MacArthur issues General Order No. 1.
- August 18, 1945 – Soviet Army invades Karafuto on southern Sakhalin Island.
- August 18, 1945 – Soviet amphibious landings in northern Korea.
- August 18, 1945 – Soviet invasion of the Kuril Islands begins with amphibious landings on Shumshu.[1]
- August 19, 1945 – Kwantung Army HQ transmit capitulation order to Japanese troops in Manchuria.
- August 23, 1945 – Last Japanese troops on Shumshu surrender to Soviet forces.[2]
- August 25, 1945 – Japanese surrender in Karafuto (south Sakhalin Island).
- August 27, 1945 – B-29s drop supplies to Allied POWs in China.
- **August 28, 1945 – U.S. troops land near Tokyo to begin the occupation of Japan.**
- August 29, 1945 – The Soviets shoot down a B-29 Superfortress dropping supplies to POWs in Korea
- August 30, 1945 – The United Kingdom reoccupies Hong Kong.
- **September 2, 1945– Japanese surrender ceremony on USS *Missouri* in Tokyo Bay; Pres. Harry S. Truman declares VJ Day.**
- September 3, 1945 – The Japanese commander Gen. Yamashita, surrenders to Gen. Wainwright at Baguio.
- September 4, 1945 – Japanese troops on Wake Island surrender.
- September 5, 1945 – The British land in Singapore.
- September 5, 1945 – The Soviets complete their occupation of the Kuril Islands.[3]
- **September 8, 1945– MacArthur enters Tokyo.**
- September 8, 1945 – U.S. forces land at Incheon to occupy Korea south of the 38th Parallel
- September 9, 1945 – Japanese in Korea surrender.
- September 13, 1945 – Japanese in Burma surrender.
- [Sept. 27, 1945 – John arrives in Tokyo Harbor]
- October 25, 1945 – Japanese in Taiwan surrender to Generalissimo Chiang Kai-shek, for the political status of Taiwan.
- 1945-1989 - 23 different "Japanese holdouts" continue from 1945-49 [6], 1950s [8], 1960s [2], 1970s [4], 1980-89 [3].

Bombing Raids in Japan: March 9 - June 15, 1945

Raid #	Date	Cities	B-29's	Lost	Damaged	Bombs	Deaths	Buildings lost	Area [sq. mi.]	Notes
1	1945/03/09	Tokyo #1	334	14	40	1700 tons incen.	100,000	167,171	15.8	3 hour raid; total d/bdg
2	1945/03/11	Nagoya #1	313	1	20	[1565 tons]	0	0	2	
3	1945/03/13	Osaka #1	274	2	13	[1370 tons]	4,666	134,944	8	3 hour raid
4	1945/03/16	Kobe	[250]			[1250 tons]	8,841	65,961	3	Japanese fighters
5	1945/03/19	Nagoya #2	[250]			[1250 tons]	0	0	3	
6	1945/04/07	Tokyo #2	[250]			[1250 tons]	0	0	11.4	
7	1945/04/15	Tokyo #3	303	12		[1500 tons]	0	102,317	6	
7	1945/04/15	Kawasaki				[2000 tons]	0	31,603	3.6	
7	1945/04/15	Yokohama #1				[2000 tons]	0	15,000	1.5	
8	1945/05/14	Nagoya #3	471	10		2515 tons incen.	0	0	3.15	18 Japanese fighters lost
9	1945/05/16	Nagoya #4	457			3609 tons	3,869	113,460	3.82	
10	1945/05/23	Tokyo #4	520			[4100 tons]	0	0	5.3	
11	1945/05/25	Tokyo #5	502			[3000 tons]	0	0	16.8	[6 raids equalled 56.3 sq. mi]
12	1945/05/26-6/4	Yokohama #2	517			[4085 tons]	0	0	6.9	150 Zekes/ P-51's destroyed 49
13	1945/05/26-6/4	Osaka #2	[400]			[2400 tons]	0	0	3.15	
14	1945/06/05	Kobe #2	530			[2400 tons]	0	51,399	4.35	
15	1945/06/07	Osaka #3	[400]			[2400 tons]	0	1000 ind.	2.21	
16	1945/06/15	Osaka #4				[3500 tons]	0		1.9	
17	1945/06/15	Amagasaki	500				0	severe	0.6	
		TOTALS	6960	136		41,592 tons	333,000 deaths			

	Date	City	B-29's	Lost	Damaged	Bombs				
	1945/08/06	Hiroshima	1/7	0		141 lbs U-235/ 4.85 tons 16,000 tons of force	day 1: 80,000; day 2-120: +80,000 of 350,000 residents * 31 **not dropped** * or used			
	1945/08/09	Nagasaki	1/6	0		14 lbs Pl / 5.15 tons 21,000 tons of force	day 1: 40,000; day 2-120: +40,000 of 263,000 people [249,000+12,500 Koreans+600 Chinese+400 Allied POWs * 119 **not dropped** * or used			

NOTE: There were 150 nuclear bombs built that were *not* used at the end of the war

Partial list of B-29 bombing missions against Tokyo

- 19 February 1945: 119 B-29s hit port and urban area
- 25 February 1945: 174 B-29s dropping incendiaries destroy ~28,000 buildings
- 4 March 1945: 159 B-29s hit urban area
- 10 March 1945: 334 B-29s dropping incendiaries destroy ~267,000 buildings; ~25% of city (*Operation Meetinghouse*) killing some 100,000
- 2 April 1945: >100 B-29s bomb the Nakajima aircraft factory
- 3 April 1945: 68 B-29s bomb the Koizumi aircraft factory and urban areas in Tokyo
- 7 April 1945: 101 B-29s bomb the Nakajima aircraft factory.
- 13 April 1945: 327 B-29s bomb the arsenal area
- 15 April 1945: 109 B-29s hit urban area
- 24 May 1945: 520 B-29s bomb urban-industrial area south of the Imperial Palace
- 26 May 1945: 464 B-29s bomb urban area immediately south of the Imperial Palace
- 20 July 1945: 1 B-29 drops a Pumpkin bomb (bomb with same ballistics as the Fat Man nuclear bomb) through overcast aiming at but missing the Imperial Palace. The dropping of Pumpkin Bombs of other sites continued on July 23, July 26, July 29, Aug. 8 and Aug. 14 [49 bombs on 14 different targets in six strikes].
- *6 August 1945: 1 B-29 bomb drop of the Fat Man over Hiroshima.*
- 8 August 1945: ~60 B-29s bomb the aircraft factory and arsenal
- *9 August 1945: 1 B-29 bomb drop of the Little Boy over Nagasaki*
- 10 August 1945: 70 B-29s bomb the arsenal complex
- 14 August 1945: final drop of a Pumpkin bomb

WORLD WAR II Deaths

Country	Enemy	Total deaths
Albania	Germany	30,000
Armenia	Germany	180,000
Austria	Germany	120,000
Azerbaijan	Germany	300,000
Belarus	Germany	2,290,000
Belgium	Germany	88,000
Brazil	Germany	2,000
Bulgaria	Germany	25,000
Canada	Germany	45,400
Cuba	Germany	100
Czechoslovakia	Germany	325,000
Denmark	Germany	3,200
Estonia	Germany	50,000
Ethiopia	Germany	100,000
Finland	Germany	97,000
France	Germany	550,000
Georgia	Germany	300,000
Greece	Germany	795,100
Hungary	Germany	580,000
Iceland	Germany	200
Iran	Germany	200
Iraq	Germany	500
Ireland	Germany	10,200
Kazakhstan	Germany	660,000
Kyrgyzstan	Germany	120,000
Latvia	Germany	230,000
Lithuania	Germany	350,000
Luxembourg	Germany	2,000
Malta (British)	Germany	1,500
Mexico	Germany	100
Moldova	Germany	170,000
Netherlands	Germany	301,000
Newfoundland (UK)	Germany	100
Norway	Germany	9,500
Poland	Germany	5,820,000
Romania	Germany	800,000
Ruanda-Urundi (Bel.)	Germany	300,000
Russia	Germany	13,950,000
South Africa	Germany	11,900
Soviet Union	Germany	[see countries]
Sweden	Germany	600
Switzerland	Germany	100
Tajikistan	Germany	120,000
Turkey	Germany	200
Turkmenistan	Germany	100,000
Ukraine	Germany	6,850,000
Unidentified	Germany	295,000
Uzbekistan	Germany	550,000
Yugoslavia	Germany	1,846,000
United Kingdom	Both	450,900
United States	Both	419,000
Australia	Japan	40,400
Burma (British)	Japan	1,272,000
Cambodia	Japan	1,200,000
China	Japan	20,000,000
Dutch East Indies	Japan	4,000,000
French Indochina	Japan	2,000,000
Guam	Japan	2,000
India (British)	Japan	1,000,000
Indonesian	Japan	1,600,000
Korea (Japan. Col.)	Japan	483,000
Malaya (British)	Japan	1,200,000
Mongolia	Japan	300
Nauru (Australian)	Japan	500
Nepal	Japan	[with UK]
New Zealand	Japan	11,900
Papua/New Guinea	Japan	15,000
Philippines (U.S.)	Japan	2,057,000
Portuguese Timor	Japan	70,000
Singapore (British)	Japan	50,000
South Pacific Mandate	Japan	57,000
Thailand	Japan	7,600
Vietnamese	Japan	1,200,000
Europeans [general]	USSR	7,640,000
Germany	Allies	9,000,000
Italy	Allies	454,600
Japan	Allies	3,120,000
TOTALS		**95,731,100**

INDEX

[name] = married name; { } = information; (name) = maiden name

Item	Page
#	
"Abilene Town"	189, 203
"Along Came Jones"	189, 200
"Anna and the King of Siam"	189, 194
"Bad Girls"	189, 193
"Bedside Manner"	189, 199
"Behind the Green Lights"	189, 198
"Captain Kidd"	189, 202
"China Sky"	189
"Cinderella Jones"	189
"Colonel Effingham's Raid"	189, 194
"Cornered"	189, 194
"Diamond Horseshoe"	189, 195
"Don Juan Quilligan"	189
"Dragon Seed"	189, 197
"Dragonwyck"	189, 190
"Gilda"	189, 192
"Her Highness and the Bellboy"	189
"Here Come the Co-eds"	189, 195
"Hold That Blonde"	189
"In This Our Life" {1942}	189, 195
"Johnny Angel"	189
"Keys of the Kingdom"	189, 202
"Kiss and Tell"	189
"Leave Her to Heaven"	189, 200
"Life with Blondie"	189
"Little Giant"	189, 200
"Our Vines Have Tender Grapes"	189, 199
"Panama Hattie"	189
"Practically Yours"	189
"Rhapsody in Blue"	189, 190
"Salome, Where She Danced"	189, 199
"San Antonio"	189, 198
"Saratoga Trunk"	189, 197
"Scared Stiff"	189, 194
"Scarlet Street"	189, 198
"Southern"	189
"Spellbound"	189, 199
"State Fair"	189, 193
"Summer Storm"	189, 190
"Swing Parade of 1946"	189, 202

"Tars & Spars"	189
"Tarzan and the Green Goddess"	189, 196
"Ten Cents a Dance"	189
"The ABC's of the USA"	189
"The Bandit of Sherwood Forest"	189, 191
"The Big Sleep"	189, 191
"The Blue Dahlia"	189, 193
"The Body Snatcher"	189, 200
"The Dark Corner"	189, 196
"The Dolly Sisters"	189, 196
"The Harvey Girls"	189, 196
"The Mask of Diljon"	189, 198
"The Postman Always Rings Twice"	189, 203
"The Sailor takes a Wife"	189
"The Spiral Staircase"	189, 197
"The Stork Club"	189, 203
"The Valley of Decision"	189, 191
"The Wife of Monte Cristo"	189, 192
"They Were Expendable"	189, 195
"Thrill of a Romance"	189, 202
"Tin Pan Alley"	189
"Two Sisters From Boston"	189, 191
"Unashamed"	189
"Under the Sun"	189
"Up Goes Maisie"	189, 192
"Week-end at the Waldorf"	189, 193
"Weekend Pass"	189
"Wilson"	189, 192
"Within These Walls"	189, 203
"Ziegfeld Follies"	189, 197
?, Andy	99
?, Anita	62, 133, 139
?, Ann	66, 83, 95
?, Ann Louise	82, **89**
?, Avery	149, 159
?, Betty Rae	123
?, Billie	123, 125
?, Blair	165
?, Breson	153
?, Charlie {sailor}	143
?, Cotton	185
?, Dan	159
?, Deffie	185
?, Fish	77
?, George	153, 185
?, Greta	62, 123
?, Hank	187

?, Helen {French}	125
?, Ira	125
?, Jane	123, 125
?, Jimmy	149, 165
?, John	185
?, June	66, 105
?, Kataki	62, 109
?, Katsu Ha	62, 99
?, Katuka	99
?, Kelly	125
?, Larry	139, 153, 169, 180
?, Madrir Marie	180
?, Marie	165
?, Mary	125, 129, 133, 139
?, Mary [Brochowler]	see: Brochowler, Mary (?)
?, Mary Ann	83, 89, 111, 119, 133
?, Millie	185
?, Miss Mickey	174, 180
?, Oliver	185
?, Patricia [Mull]	204
?, Peggy	143
?, Skippy	66, 133
?, Stuck	153, 165
?, Takeo	133
?, Tinsy	66, 123
?, Tomi	62
?, Tootsie	149
?, Totsi	133, 139, 165, 169, 174, 180, 185
?, Wade	91
?, Wyatt	125
155mm artillery	vi
207 Kimrod Lane, Charlotte, NC	vii
2800 Shenandoah Avenue, Charlotte, NC	vii, 225
3300 Winterfield Place, Charlotte, NC	vii, 247, 248
369th Field Artillery, US Army	vi
98th Division, US Army	vi

A

Ainsworth {ship}	174
Alberta	vi
Alexander, Gen. Harold	72
Almer, R.I.	66
Amagaski, Japan	72
Amboy, MN	62
Ambrose, Helen	169
Araki, Gen. Sadao	177, 178
Arkansas	64
Assembly Inn, Montreat, NC	240
Atkins, Sue Anna (Carriker)	see: Carriker, Sue Anna [Atkins]
Atkins, Tommy	83
Atsugi Airfield, Japan	123, 129, 133
Austin, TX	64
Austria	72

B

B., Norma	66
B., Ruth	119
B-29	70
Baldison, Gloria	62, 83, 95, 123, 153, 187
Baltimore, MD	64
Barefoot, Loretta Jean	17
Barium Springs Orphanage	vi, 3, 5
Barium Springs, NC	3
Bat Cave, NC	32, 78, 217, 218
Battle of Berlin	72
Battle of the Bulge, Belgium	68
Bavaria	72
Berrios, Dorothy (Mull)	see: Mull, Dorothy [Berrios]
Billew, ?	165
Blackwelder, Columbus	2
Blackwelder, Esther Hartsell	see: Hartsell, Esther [Blackwelder]
Blackwelder, Vernina Lenora [Carriker]	2, 7
Blakey, ?	125
Bogart, Humphrey	129
bombing raids in Japan	100
Boston, MA	62
Boutewell, Chaplain John L. {MS}	119
Bradley, Jane	159
Braught, Lt. ?	83
Brazil	259
Brindel, Miss ?	174
British Columbia	vi
Brochowler, Mary ?	62, 66, 116, 117, 140

Brown Presbytery, PCUS	6
Buddha Statue, Komakura {Diabutsu}	40, 138, 163, 174
Bull, Ruth	66, 83
Burke, ?	95
Butler, James	62

C

Caldwell Memorial Pres. Ch., Charlotte, NC	vii, 6
California	vi
Camp Bennett	121
Camp Hood, TX	60-64, 68
Camp Mardin, Japan	121
Camp Meade, MD	65
Caney, KS	62
Canteen girl	62
Carman, Howard	62
Carolina Beach, NC	213
Carriker, Adam Timothy, Jr.	2
Carriker, Alma Elizabeth (Dorsey)	see: Dorsey, Alma Elizabeth [Carriker]
Carriker, Alpha Lafayette, Jr.	4, 236
Carriker, Alpha Lafayette, Sr.	2, 7
Carriker, Anabel	v, 263, 267
Carriker, Annie (Taylor)	see: Taylor, Annie [Carriker]
Carriker, Ashleigh Kristen	v, 253, 267
Carriker, Charles Timothy, Jr.	v, 258, 263, 264, 267
Carriker, Charles Timothy, Sr.	v, 237-239, 241-243, 245, 247
"	257-259, 263-265, 267
Carriker, Donald Malloy	v, 6, 13, 17, 28, 30, 32, 33, 36, 61, 62
"	66, 68, 87, 109, 187, 212, 241
Carriker, Dorothy Jane [Hall]	32, 216, 236
Carriker, Gene	62, 66
Carriker, Jack Anderson	v, 260, 267
Carriker, Jane Marie Owen	3
Carriker, Jeffrey Stewart	18
Carriker, Jennifer Cristina Kerr [Lauria]	v, 257, 265, 267
Carriker, John Anderson, III	v, 233-239, 241, 245, 247, 260, 267
Carriker, John Anderson, IV	v, 251, 252, 260, 267
Carriker, John Anderson, Jr.	the entire book
Carriker, John Anderson, Sr.	v, vi, vii, 1, 2, 10, 11, 12, 13, 17, 27,
"	30, 33, 36, 62, 63, 68, 82, 83, 87, 89,
"	95, 109, 119, 165, 187, 236, 240
Carriker, Jonathan Michael	v, 254, 261, 267
Carriker, Jonathan Paul	v, 261, 267
Carriker, Joseph Paul	v, 255, 267
Carriker, Joyce Leigh (Henry)	see: Henry, Joyce Leigh [Carriker] {Burns}
Carriker, Kimberley Diane	18

Carriker, Laura Belle	95
Carriker, Lauren Elizabeth (Cook)	see: Cook, Lauren Elizabeth [Carriker]
Carriker, Liseth (Figeuro)	See: Figeuro, Liseth [Carriker]
Carriker, Lois Elizabeth [Clark]	v, vi, 6, 13, 14, 15, 16, 25, 27, 30, 33
"	62, 68, 83, 89111, 187, 229
Carriker, Marcelo	v, 264, 267
Carriker, Marta (Kerr)	see: Kerr, Marta [Carriker]
Carriker, Merrell Berneice (Mull)	see: Mull, Merrell Berneice [Carriker]
Carriker, Michael Anderson	18
Carriker, Michelle (Gray)	see: Gray, Michelle [Carriker]
Carriker, Rebekah Joyce [Motley]	v, 255, 256, 262, 267
Carriker, Richard Donald	v, 237-239, 241, 244, 245, 247, 267
Carriker, Samuel David, Jr.	v, 252, 267
Carriker, Samuel David, Sr.	v, 17, 236-239, 241, 245, 247, 255,
"	261, 262, 267
Carriker, Sandra (Crump)	see: Crump, Sandra [Carriker]
Carriker, Sarah Kerr	v, 259, 267
Carriker, Shannan (Pulley)	see: Pulley, Shannan [Carriker]
Carriker, Sue Anna [Atkins]	4, 66, 83, 119, 133
Carriker, Vernina Lenora (Blackwelder)	see: Blackwelder, Vernina Lenora [Carriker]
Cartwright, Chaplain ?	139
Caserta, Italy	72
Caskey, Sgt. Clyde J, {KS}	109, 113, 119-121
Central High School	221, 222
Chapin family, Neudorf, Saskatchewan, CAN	vi, 6
Charlotte, NC	vii, 2, 6, 15, 17, 60, 62, 187
Chicago, IL	62, 187
Chimney Rock, NC	82
Chipley Avenue, Charlotte, NC	6
Chnooski, Clements	62
Christensen, Bob	62
Church {intact} in Yokohama, Japan	150
Cincinnati, OH	62
Clark, Carol Ann [O'Brien]	16, 187, 233, 236
Clark, Edmund Burke	6, 16, 68, 89, 111, 236
Clark, Laura Elizabeth	13, 16, 236
Clark, Lois Elizabeth (Carriker)	see: Carriker, Lois Elizabeth [Clark]
Clifton, KS	vi, 6, 12-14, 20
Columbus, OH	62
Commonwealth Pres. Ch., Charlotte, NC	6
Concord Presbytery, PCUS	6
Concord, NC	6
Cook, Lauren Elizabeth [Carriker]	267
Couchell, George, I	204
Couchell, Theophanis [Robinson]	204
Cove Presbyterian Church, Weirton, WV	6

Covington, Dave & Elsie (McLauchlin)	254
Cowart, ?	66
Crainley, Howard	62
Crausby, ?	83
Crump, Sandra [Carriker]	251, 260, 267

D

Dallas, TX	62, 64
Daly, Capt. ?	62, 121
Darnell, Elizabeth [McIntire]	see: McIntire, Elizabeth (Darnell)
Davidson College	vi, 3, 4, 7
Deatherage, Judy (Ratledge)	see: Ratledge, Judy [Deatherage]
DeCarlo, Yvonne	79
Delaware	64
Denmark	72
Denton, Ella [Dorsey]	236
Detroit, MI	64, 68
Devine, Leo C.	62, 95
Diabutsu Temple	44-47, 51
Dill, Dorothy {Rockette}	149
Doihara, Gen. Kenji	177
Dole Pineapple Plant, HI	76, 79
Dönitz, Admiral Karl	72
Dorsey, Alma Elizabeth [Carriker]	v, vi, 7, 8, 9, 10, 12, 13, 14, 17, 27, 30,
"	32, 33, 36, 61, 62, 68, 82, 83, 87, 89,
"	95, 109, 165, 187, 236, 237, 240, 250
Dorsey, C.F.	83
Dorsey, Ella (Denton)	see: Denton, Ella [Dorsey]
Dorsey, Frances Sarah (Strode)	see: Strode, Frances Sarah [Dorsey]
Dorsey, Jimmy	78
Dorsey, Mabel Frank [McGuire]	30, 66
Dorsey, Margeret (McIntire)	see: McIntyre, Margaret [Dorsey]
Dorsey, Margaret Clarene [Gillespie]	30, 89
Dorsey, Samuel William	10, 11, 12, 27, 30, 236
Dorsey, Sarah Elizabeth (Howe)	see: Howe, Sarah Elizabeth [Dorsey]
Dorsey, William David {Buddy}	30
Dorsey, William Ingram	11
Dugan, Mrs.	66
Dunlap, Jane [Howe]	8
Dunlap, Sarah [Howe]	8
Dunlap, Sarah Jane [Howe]	see: Howe, Sarah Jane (Dunlap)
Durbin, Deanna	129

E

Earle Theatre, Washington, DC	62, 72
East Side Pres. Chapel, Charlotte, NC	vii, 6
Eastminster Pres. Chapel, Charlotte, NC	6
Eastminster Pres. Church, Charlotte, NC	vii, 6, 15, 17, 216, 225, 226, 244
Ebenezer Presbytery, UPCUSA	6
Eisenhower, Gen. Dwight	72, 143, 171
Eldorado Pres. Church, Eldorado, TX	vi, 6, 36
Eldorado, TX	vi, 6, 36, 37, 60, 61, 68, 244
Elizaville Cemetery, Elizaville, KY	11
Elizaville Pres. Church, Elizaville, KY	vi, 6
Elizaville, KY	vi, 6, 8, 9, 10, 27
Emporer's Palace, Tokyo	154, 155, 171
Engel, Clarence	62, 79
Enoshima, Japan	64, 130, 156, 159-162, 180, 185
Erie Railroad	35, 37
Euitah, PFC ?	185
Europe	vi

F

Farmer, ?	153, 165, 174, 185
Fayetteville, NC	187
Figeuro, Liseth [Carriker]	263, 264, 267
Finland	72
First Pres. Church, Clifton, KS	vi, 6, 20
First Pres. Church, Hopkins, MO	vi, 6
First Pres. Church, Redding, CA	vi, 6
Forest Lawn Pres. Church, Marion, OH	vi, 6, 24, 28, 33
Fort Bragg, NC	60, 187
Fort Hall, HI	64
Fort Hood, TX	75, 87
Fort Hose, HI	60
Fort Lawton, WA	60, 64, 71, 72, 187
Fort Meade, MD	60, 72, 87
Fort Plose, HA	83
Fort Sam Houston, TX	60, 61, 68, 87
Fort Wilderness, Walt Disney World, FL	256
Fort Worth, TX	62, 64, 65, 68
Foster, Miss. ?	169
Fostoria, OH	187
Furguson, ?	121

G

Gagloid, ?	99
Germany	72
Geta shoes	127, 152
Gillespie, Margaret Clarene (Dorsey)	see: Dorsey, Margaret Clarene [Gillespie]
Gillespie, Richard Dorsey	30
Gillespie, Uncle Cecil	30, 66, 89
Giulino, Italy	72
Glen Echo Park, MD	62, 64, 67, 72
Goebbels, Joseph	72
Gordon, Richard & Nancy (?)	213-215
Göring, Hermann	72
Grace, Crizie	68
Grace, Norma	68
Gray, Michelle [Carriker]	267

H

Hachiman Shrine	48
Hall, Dorothy Jane (Carriker)	see: Carriker, Dorothy Jane [Hall]
Hall, Wayne	236
Hamilton, Norma [Mull]	223
Hamilton, Stewart	62
Handell, Capt. ?	62, 109, 111, 115
Handy, Mary Gene {Candy}	62, 72
Hare, Bud {VA}	62, 87
Harrington, John	62
Harrisburg, NC	6
Hartsell, Esther [Blackwelder]	2
Hashimoto, Col. Kingiro	177
Hata, Field Marshall Shunroku	177
Hawaii	64, 73, 78
Hay, Ruth	62, 66, 83, 89
Helemano, Oahu, HI	60, 76
Henry, Joyce Leigh [Carriker] {Burns}	261, 262, 267
Hickam Field, HI	64, 87
Hickory Nut Falls, Chimney Rock, NC	82
Hicks, Lt. ?	99, 111
Hiranuma, Baron Kiichiro	177
Hiroshima, Japan	77, 176
Hirota, Prime Minister Koki	177
Hitler, Adolf	72
Hitler, Eva (Braun)	72
Hodge, ?	180, 185
Hoffman, Lt. ?	99, 105, 111
Hohenberger, Leonard	62, 83, 121, 133
Honey Wagon	130

Honolulu, HI	64, 72, 76, 78, 81, 83-86
Honshu Island, Japan	87
Hope, Maj. ?	165
Hopkins, MO	vi, 6
Hoshino, Politician Naoki	177
Hottie, Bob	159
Houghton, Jean {Jane, sister to John}	66, 68
Houghton, Jim {brother to John}	68, 119, 140
Houghton, Lt. John {B-29}	139, 140
Houghton, Mrs. ? {mother of John, Jim & Jane}	140
Howe, David	8
Howe, David Washington	10
Howe, Jane (Dunlap)	see: Dunlap, Jane [Howe]
Howe, John	8
Howe, John David	8, 10
Howe, Sarah (Dunlap)	see: Dunlap, Sarah [Howe]
Howe, Sarah Elizabeth [Dorsey]	10, 11, 13, 27, 30
Howe, Sarah Jane (Dunlap)	8, 10
Howell, MI	62
Huffman House	204
Huffman, Inez [?]	204
Huffman, Peggy Triby [Mull]	204
Hunterville Pres. Ch., Hunterville, Alberta, CAN	vi, 6
Hunterville, Alberta, CAN	vi, 6
Hyde, Capt. ?	83, 109

I

Ice skating at Texas Christian University	64
Idaho	64
Illinois	64
Imperial Hotel, Tokyo, Japan	124, 132, 134
Imperial Palace, Tokyo, Japan	76
Indian Soldiers	147, 155
Indian Trail Pres. Ch., Indian Trail, NC	vii, 6, 212, 224
Indian Trail, NC	vii, 6, 224
Indiana	64
Iowa	64, 187
Ischigawa, Japan	90
Itagaki, Gen. Seishiro	177
Italy	72
Iwo Jima	68

J

Japan	vi, 69, 76, 77, 80, 87, 89, 181
Japan, Map of	181
Japanes girls	164
Japanese Aircraft Carrier	93
Japanese Baby	151
Japanese boys	164
Japanese family	152
Japanese Jailbirds	141
Japanese Mother	151
Japanese priests	166
Jenkins, Philip	62
Jodl, Gen. Alfred	72
Johnston, Lt. ?	99
Jordan, Sgt. ?	115
Junior, Jack	119

K

Kamakure, Japan	48, 64, 159, 163, 167, 169, 174
Kansas	vi
Kansas City, MO	62
Kawasaki, Japan	68, 93
Kaya, Min. Okinori	177
Keitel, Gen. Wilhelm	72
Kentucky	vi
Kerr, Marta [Carriker]	257-259, 263-265, 267
Key West, FL	250
Kido, Marq. Koichi	177
Kimura, Gen. Yasushi	177
Kinlon, PA	62
Kirkland, Mrs. ?	169
Knox Pres. Ch., Terrace, British Columbia, CAN	vi, 6
Kobe, Japan	64, 68
Koiso, Gen. Kuniaki	177
Komakura, Japan	138
Koriyama, Japan	60
Kure, Japan	148
Kyoto, Japan	49, 64, 143

L

Lake Wylie, SC	213-215
Lakewood Gamily Campground	247
Lancaster County, SC	8
Latta Park, NC	219, 220, 223
Lattimore, Sgt.	62
Lauria, Gabrielle Kairi Carriker	v, 265, 267
Lauria, Jennifer Cristina Kerr (Carriker)	see: Carriker, Jennifer Cristina Kerr [Lauria]
Lauria, Michael	265, 267
Ledy, ?	83
Lesbon, OH	129
Lewis, Maj. ?	99
Liberty troop ship	60, 71
Lida, Sgt. Jack	83
Lincoln, NB	187
Lindel, Gummer	105
Lindu, Grant	62, 66, 68
Litwin, Lou {USO}	149
Loome, Gen. James Thomas	105
Louisville Theological Seminary	vi, 4, 5, 6
Lowry, ?	149
Lucas, Sis	62, 125, 129, 133, 139

M

Maiko girls	49
Maila, Philippines	168
Maizuru Naval Base, Japan	106
Mamiya camera	169, 170
Manhattan Project	76
Manila, Philippines	57
Mardin, 1st Lt. Clayton L.	105, 106, 121
Marion, OH	vi, 6, 17, 23-37, 62, 68, 140
Maryland	64
Mathews, Capt. Seale	62
Matsui, Gen. Iwane	177
Matsuoka, Dip. Yosuke	177
Matsusake, Japan	60, 115, 119
McArthur, Arthur, IV	124
McArthur, Gen. Douglas	124, 134, 143, 171
McArthur, Mrs. Jean Marie (Faircloth)	123
McClelland, Mrs. ?	174
McGuire, Mabel Frank (Dorsey)	see: Dorsey, Mabel Frank [McGuire]
McIntire, Duskin	9, 10
McIntire, Elizabeth (Darnell)	9, 10, 13
McIntyre, Margaret [Dorsey]	10
McNutt, Paul	76

Meagis, Sgt. ?	111
Mecklenburg House, Montreat, NC	6, 230, 231
Mecklenburg Presbytery, PCUS	6
Medford, Kay {actress}	139
Meehon, Miss Ruth	62, 125, 133, 159, 165, 169, 180, 185
Meiji Building, Tokyo	157
Methodist Children's Home, Winston-Salem, NC	vii, 205-209
Michigan	64
Miller, Maggie	125
Minami, Gen. Jiro	177
Minnesota	vi, 14, 64, 187
Missoula, MT	187
Missouri	vi, 64
Montana	vi, 64
Montgomery, Gen. Bernard	133
Montreat, NC	230, 231, 240
Morganton, NC	vii
Morris Field Pres. Chapel, Charlotte, NC	vii, 6
Morris, ?	121
Motley, Ben	262, 267
Motley, Hannah Elizabeth	v, 262, 267
Motley, Rebekah Joyce (Carriker)	see: Carriker, Rebekah Joyce [Motley]
Mount Fuji {Fujiyama}	50, 178, 184
Mt. Ranier, WA	72
Mull, Calvin	204-210, 223, 230
Mull, Cloye Jane [Mull]	204
Mull, Dorothy [Berrios]	204, 230
Mull, H.J.	209
Mull, Marvin Wesley	204, 230
Mull, Merrell Berneice [Carriker]	v, vii, 15, 204-211, 213-221, 226,
"	228-230, 233, 235-237, 241, 242,
"	245-247, 249-251, 255, 260-265, 267
Mull, Monroe	209
Mull, Norma (Hamilton)	see: Hamilton, Norma [Mull]
Mull, Patricia	204
Mull, Patricia (?)	see: ?, Patricia [Mull]
Mull, Peggy Triby (Huffman)	see: Huffman, Peggy Triby [Mull]
Mull, Ruth [Ratledge]	204, 230
Mull, Shirley	204, 230
Mull, Wesley	204
Mull, Wilson	230
Murphy, George {USO}	78
Mussolini, Benito	72
Muto, Gen. Akira	177, 178
Myrtle Beach State Park	240, 245, 246
Myrtle Beach, SC	242

N

Nadeau, Miss ?	165, 180
Nagano, Adm. Osami	177
Nagasaki, Japan	77, 98
Nagoya, Japan	60, 64, 68, 93, 119
Nara, Japan	44-47, 51-54, 60, 62, 64, 95, 97, 99,
"	105-108, 111, 112, 115, 119, 121, 122
Nebraska	187
Nelson, Jenny	253
Nelson, Jim	133
Nesbitt, Maj. ?	121
Netherlands	72
Neudorf, Saskatchewan, CAN	vi, 6
New Mexico	76
New York	62
North Carolina	vii, 169
North Dakota	64
Numagawa, Japan	50

O

O'Brien, Carol Ann (Clark)	see: Clark, Carol Ann [O'Brien]
O'Neil, Bill	62
Oahu, Hawaii	60, 74, 80, 85, 121
Octogon Theatre	140, 165
Ohio	vi, 64
Oka, Adm. Takasumi	177, 178
Okasaki, Japan	64
Okawa, Politician Shumei	177, 178
Okazaki, Japan	64
Okinawa, Japan	68
Okuma, Min. Hiroki	177
Old Mexico, TX	64
old Waxhaw, SC	8
O'Neil, Bill	83
Orr, Lt.	62
Osaka, Japan	52, 60, 64, 68, 87, 91, 93, 95-97, 99,
"	104, 108, 109, 111, 112, 119, 121,
Oshima, Gen. Hiroshi	177
Ostrium, Johnny {USO}	149
Oven Auditorium, Charlotte, NC	244
Owen, Jane Marie [Carriker]	see: Carriker, Jane Marie (Owen)
Ozakai, Japan	60

P

Pacific Landings by US forces	70
Pacific Ocean	78
Pali Pass on Oahu, HI	64, 78
Patterson, John	62
Pearl Harbor, HI	64, 82
Pennsylvania	64
Philippines	57, 73
Phillips, Mr. ?	139
Poolent, Barbara June	89
Porter, ?	169
Potsdam Declaration	77
Presbyterian Church of Canada	6
Presbyterian Church, United States	6
Presbytery of Marion-Portsmouth, UPCUSA	6
Presbytery of Topeka-Wichita, UPCUSA	6
Presbytery of Wheeling-Chippewa, UPCUSA	6
President Roosevelt	68
Presley, Bob	83, 123, 125, 133, 139, 143, 149, 153, 159, 165, 169, 174, 180
Pulley, Shannan [Carriker]	260, 267
Pumpkin Bomb	76
Punaluu tidal wave	146
Punaluu, Oahu, HI	60, 64, 73, 76, 77, 80, 82, 146
Pyle, Ernie	153, 154, 169

R

Ratledge, Judy [Deatherage]	210
Ratledge, Ruth (Mull)	see: Mull, Ruth [Ratledge]
Red Cross	vii, 62, 66, 97, 109, 111, 117, 119, 121, 123, 125, 134, 140
Redding, CA	vi, 6
Reese, Tech. Sgt. ?	119, 120, 122
Riccardi, ?	165, 174
Richardson, Gen.	76
Robinson, Theophanis (Couchell)	see: Couchell, Theophanis [Robinson]
Rocky Ridge United Methodist Church	2
Rocky River Presbyterian Church	3
Rogers, Tara	261, 267
Rose, Kimberley Diane (Carriker)	see: Carriker, Kimberley Diane [Rose]
Royal Gurkha Army	148
Ruderick, ?	95
Ryugasaki, Japan	143

S

S.S. Cape Johnson {liberty troop ship}	64, 79, 91
S.S. John W. Brown {liberty troop ship}	71
S.S. Julian {liberty troop ship}	60, 64, 72
S.S. Norway Victory {victory troop ship}	60, 185, 186
Saiban, Japan	90
Saipan	60, 64, 87, 89
Sakai, Japan	99
Sallicorn, ?	165
Samurai Family	41, 42
San Angelo, TX	64, 68
San Antonio, TX	62, 64, 68
Sanford, NC	60, 187
Saskatchewan	vi
Sato, Gen. Kenryo	177
Sawyer, Mary Ann	62, 66
Schofield Barracks, HI	82, 83, 85
Seattle, WA	60, 64, 71, 72, 185-187
Sendai, Japan	139
Sheffield barracks, HI	64
Shigemitsu, Min. Mamoru	177
Shimada, Adm. Shigetaro	177
Shiratori, Amb. Toshio	177
Shomu, Emporer	44
Shōwa, Emporer Hirohito	123, 153
Siler Presbyterian Church, Wesley Chapel, NC	vii, 6, 224
Simon, Maj. ?	62, 111, 119, 121
Sledge, Ginny {Charlotte}	169
Slegle, Virginia	62, 82
Smith, Cora	139
Smith, Dorothy	62, 82
Smith, Mary	123
Smith, Pat {actress}	62, 143, 153
Smithsonian Museum	64
Snead, Jack	187
Snyder, ?	109
South Dakota	64
Spiner, ?	121
Spokane, WA	77
St. Andrews Epis. Ch., Yokohama, Japan	136, 137
St. Joseph Presbytery, UPCUSA	6
Stack, Bob	125
Stillwell, Gen. Joseph Warren {d. 1946}	91
Stitt, ?	121
Strode, Frances Sarah [Dorsey]	11
Suzuka, Japan	60
Suzuki, Gen. Teiichi	177

T

Taisho Air Field, Osaka, Japan	60, 64, 96, 97, 99
Tanbanbi, Japan	111
Tanbrach, Japan	60
Taylor, Annie [Carriker]	32, 66, 236
Taylor, Estelle	32
Temmoji Buddhist Temple	52
Temple grounds	167
Temple on Enoshima Island	158
Terrace, British Columbia, CAN	vi, 6
Texas	vi, 165
Texas Christian University	37, 62, 65, 68
Timpson, TX	62
Tinian Islands	64
Toba, Japan	60, 64, 115
Tochikama, Japan	123
Todd, Miss ?	62, 129, 139, 159, 165, 169
Togo, Min. Shigenori	177
Tojo, Gen. Hideki	87, 100-102, 168, 169, 177, 178
Tokyo Bay, Japan	85, 93
Tokyo, Japan	60, 64, 68, 76, 88, 90, 123-127, 129,
"	132, 134, 139, 143, 147, 149, 151-154,
"	157, 159, 165, 166, 168-172, 174, 180
"	185
Trehka, Bob	62, 159
Trout, Capt. William	103
Troutman Pres. Ch., Troutman, NC	6
Tsu, Japan	60, 64. 111. 115. 119, 121, 122, 131
Turner, Mary Ann	62, 66

U

U.S. Army	6
U.S. Army Cemetery, Yokohama, Japan	148, 181, 182
Ube, Japan	88
Ueno, Japan	115
Umezu, Gen. Yoshijiro	177, 178
Uneo Museum, Tokyo	168
Uneo Zoo, Tokyo	152
Uneo, Japan	122
Union County, NC	vii
United Presbyterian Church, USA	6
University of North Carolina	17
USS Missouri	85
USS North Carolina	69

V

Varutis, Ginger	129
Victory Parade {Army Day}	135, 171, 173, 175
Victory troop ship	60
Virginia	62
Vollmer, ?	121

W

Waianae Beach, HI	64
Waianae, Oahu, HI	60, 73, 74
Waikiki Beach, HI	64, 78
Wainwright, Gen. Jonathan, IV	57, 100
Wakayama Beach, Japan	60, 64, 80, 92, 202
Walker, Mr. ?	139
Walt Disney World	256
Walters, Hosley	62
War Crimes Trial	110
Washington	64
Washington Monument	64
Washington, DC	9, 60, 64, 72, 187
Weirton Pres. Ch., Weirton, WV	vi, 6, 21
Weirton, WV	vi, 6, 14, 21, 22
Wesley Chapel, NC	vii, 6, 224
West Virginia	vi
Williams, ?	91
Winston-Salem, NC	vii, 205-209
Wisconsin	64
Wolff, Gen. Karl	72
Wooten, Lt. Louis	62
World War I	6

Y

Yagi, Japan	109
Yamashita, Gen. Tomoyuki	57, 100, 168
Yashinara, Japan	105
Yegge, Donal	62
Yogi, Japan	60
Yokasuka, Japan	60, 185, 186
Yokohama, Japan	37-44, 54-56, 60, 64, 68, 90, 92, 94, 113, 114, 116, 117, 119, 121, 125, 128, 129, 131, 133, 136-140, 142, 144, 145, 148, 150, 152, 153, 155, 159, 165, 167, 169, 174, 179, 180, 182, 183

Z

Zimmer, Maj. W.	62, 95, 97, 99, 105, 111, 115, 119, 178

www.ingramcontent.com/pod-product-compliance
Lightning Source LLC
Chambersburg PA
CBHW062126160426
43191CB00013B/2207